WHAT THE INDUSTRY
SHOOTING BETTER MOVIES:

"Nailed it! A simple, turbo-fast read. A practical, no-nonsense, encouraging guide to filmmaking. Students of film, from the initiate to the updating pro, will enrich their knowledge and confidence with *Shooting Better Movies*. Where was this when I started?"
— PEN DENSHAM, Oscar-nominated writer, producer, director, Trilogy Entertainment Group principal, *Robin Hood: Prince of Thieves, Backdraft, Moll Flanders, Blown Away, Tank Girl, Outer Limits*

"A valuable resource for anyone starting out on their filmmaking journey."
— DR. NEIL FOX, Course Coordinator, BA (Hons) Film, Falmouth University, UK

"Dudbridge orchestrates within this do-it-yourself manual a stirring and sustained call to action: while providing a well-structured, informative guide to the essential principles and practice of filmmaking, he never stops emphasizing the importance of learning through the experiences of real-world film production. His passion and persuasiveness are equally infectious. If you are serious about making your student films stand out from their competition, you need to read this book."
— STEPHEN GORDON, Senior Lecturer in Film Production Technology, Birmingham City University (UK)

"It's refreshing to see a film book that isn't all about equipment and technical aspects. *Shooting Better Movies* covers those points, but also the feelings of a scene and the feelings of the filmmaker. A perfect blend."
— ELLIOT GROVE, founder, Raindance Film Festival, British Independent Film Awards

"An essential, jam-packed read for anyone hungry to get out there and make their movie, with tons of fun tips and advice from the author's own experiences. Highly recommended."
— EDDIE HAMILTON, film editor, *Mission: Impossible — Rogue Nation, Kingsman: The Secret Service, X-Men: First Class, Kick-Ass*

"*Shooting Better Movies* is a fantastic resource, and will be going straight to the top of my students' reading list. Key to the success of the book is Dudbridge's accessible and engaging writing style that explains, clearly and coherently, how to improve your film-making in every area. It really is a complete guide, and I can't recommend it enough."
— DR. JIMMY HAY, Lecturer in Film and Television, University of Bristol, UK

"Ever taught a class and had 'those' questions fired at you? This book answers them, and more besides. Paul's light-hearted approach, combined with real-world-useful hints and guidance, will appeal to the amateur and professional alike — and to anyone dealing with the actual reality of the filmmaking process."
— ALEX HUDD, sound recordist / post sound mixer, Dreambase Studios, UK

"What I love is that *Shooting Better Movies* doesn't just tell you how to do it, but the motivation why to do it. This wonderful resource breaks it all down for you, technique mixed with instructions how to use these skills to create emotion and feeling — the center of cinematography. If it feels right, then it's right, even if it breaks the rules! This book will make you a better storyteller."
— SHANE HURLBUT, director of photography, *Terminator Salvation*, *Need for Speed*, *Fathers and Daughters*

"This is a most informative and illuminating hands-on book with plenty of advice and technical info for both novice and student alike. Clearly set out in segments that are easy to follow . . . an excellent publication. Just start shooting, and enjoy!"
— ROGER PEARCE, camera operator, *Casino Royale*, *Goldeneye*, *Murder on the Orient Express* (2017), *Cinderella*

"As an ex-student of Paul's and having taken his workshops for years, this book contains it all! The "Secrets of Filmmaking" chapter completely changed my outlook and approach as a student, and now I'm able to work full time in the industry as a camera assistant on big shows. . . . This is a complete film school."
— SCOTT WALLER, camera assistant, *Doctor Who*, *Class*, *A Midsummer Night's Dream*, *Broadchurch*, *Stella*, and *Casualty*

Shooting BETTER Movies

THE STUDENT FILMMAKERS' GUIDE

Paul Dudbridge

MICHAEL WIESE PRODUCTIONS

Published by Michael Wiese Productions
12400 Ventura Blvd. #1111
Studio City, CA 91604
(818) 379-8799, (818) 986-3408 (FAX)
mw@mwp.com
www.mwp.com

Cover design by Johnny Ink. www.johnnyink.com
Interior design by William Morosi
Copyediting by Ross Plotkin
Printed by McNaughton & Gunn

Manufactured in the United States of America
Copyright 2017 by Paul Dudbridge

Library of Congress Cataloging-in-Publication Data

Names: Dudbridge, Paul, 1977- author.
Title: Shooting better movies : the student filmmakers' guide / Paul Dudbridge.
Description: Studio City, CA : Michael Wiese Productions, [2017]
Identifiers: LCCN 2016043614 | ISBN 9781615932719
Subjects: LCSH: Motion pictures--Production and direction--Handbooks,
  manuals, etc.
Classification: LCC PN1995.9.P7 D77 2017 | DDC 791.43/0232--dc23
LC record available at https://lccn.loc.gov/2016043614

Printed on Recycled Stock

Dedicated to all my ex-students,
who taught me more than I could ever teach you

Contents

ACKNOWLEDGMENTS

ix

HOW TO USE THIS BOOK

xi

INTRODUCTION

xiii

CHAPTER 1:

SCRIPTWRITING

1

CHAPTER 2:

PRODUCING

16

CHAPTER 3:

CAMERA AND LIGHTING

27

CHAPTER 4:

SOUND

87

CHAPTER 5:

DIRECTING, PART 1 – THE CAMERA

101

CHAPTER 6:

DIRECTING, PART 2 – ACTORS

135

CHAPTER 7:

EDITING

144

CHAPTER 8:

THREE SECRETS OF FILMMAKING

153

CHAPTER 9:

COMMON TRAITS OF STUDENT FILMS

157

CHAPTER 10:

FINAL THOUGHTS

161

SOURCES

163

ABOUT THE AUTHOR

165

Acknowledgments

This book wouldn't have been possible without the kind support, encouragement, and proofreading skills of a number of people.

First up, Simon Pearce and Will Griffin, my personal proofreaders. Simon and Will took the brunt of the early drafts and Simon had the pleasure of all the subsequent pages of notes and changes that I threw at him. They are both not only extremely talented creatives in their own right, but also have an excellent eye for spelling and grammar and are wonderful friends too.

My parents, Ken and Margaret Dudbridge, for their support and love over the years. If Dad hadn't bought that first family video camera, I don't know where I would be today. Also for their support catering the early shoots, being extras when people didn't show, and for even building my early sets in our driveway!

Jim Griffin for being a sound voice of encouragement and reminding me I'm better than I thought I was.

Roger Pearce for all your expert advice, guidance, mentorship, and technical prowess. A lot of what Roger has taught me over the years has found its way into this book, so I thank you, Roger.

To all my ex-students, who have informed me in so many ways and given me the experience to write this book, I thank you. Without you all, I wouldn't have the insight that this book needed. You've made me feel pride, joy, and happiness about all your progress and advancements. You have brought me immense satisfaction.

Mike Grant, my first mentor of sorts back in my college days. Mike taught me so many things about editing and writing that help me today. Mike also lent me his copy of *Adventures in the Screen Trade* by William Goldman, the first book about film or writing I ever read. In fact, I think I still have it, so I owe you a new copy, Mike.

Thanks to ITV Television Workshop, Bristol, and Lisa Hamilton-James. The Workshop gave me my first teaching gig back in 2004, and teaching has been a wonderful and enriching experience ever since.

Many thanks to Sam Norman for taking a selection of the photos and Alicia Ancel for modeling for them. Alan Tabrett for producing the technical illustrations and general photo touch-ups, and Andrew Lamb for his excellent storyboard work.

In no particular order, I'd also like to thank: Neil Oseman, Mark Caldwell, Colin Holloway, Eyelights Ltd, Mendip Media, Patrick Shead-Simmonds, Nicky Robertson, Priya Purmanan, Video Europe Bristol, Dave Bennett, Bill Beaumont, Julian Bray Guillaume, Bristol Old Vic Theatre School, Alex Hudd, and Dan Richardson for all your support and advice.

American Cinematographer magazine for teaching me so many things over the years. I'm glad I found that first copy back in 2006.

Finally, Pen Densham for your time and advice during our interview and for introducing me to Michael Wiese and his amazing production and publishing company, MWP. Thank you, Michael, for your supportive words and for believing in my work and this book.

How to Use This Book

This book has been written and arranged to reflect the filmmaking process: starting with scriptwriting, moving on to production, and then on to the more technical aspects of camera, sound, and editing. However, you may want to dip in and out of the various chapters, depending where your primary interest lies.

But if you consider yourself a "filmmaker," a newbie, or a more experienced jack of all trades, I'd advise you to read the book from cover to cover. You will need to know most, if not all, of the information contained herein, and to follow the order it is written.

If you're a professor or teacher, the more technical chapters on Camera and Lighting, Sound, and Editing might be good places to start. These are the nuts and bolts of filmmaking and are normally the first areas to be taught. Equally, a college or university student might start with their main area of focus or study.

For any actors reading, look at the directing chapters, specifically Directing, Part 2 — Actors. Also read the Editing chapter; it's where performances are ultimately crafted.

In the film industry, all areas and disciplines affect all others and don't work in isolation. Directors need to know a little editing, camera operators need to know some aspects of sound, editors need to know how visual effects work, and writers need to know what can be achieved by producers dealing with budgets. So even if your primary focus lies in one area, it might serve you well to know a little more about the others. You can talk their language when on set.

One final note: I like to treat my books well and with respect. However, I appreciate this is a technical manual of sorts, and you may need to highlight lines or make notes on the pages. For this one time only, if it enables you to access and remember the information more quickly, I encourage you to do so, and I'll make an exception! Enjoy.

Paul Dudbridge

July 2017

Introduction

"It's important to learn the basic grammar first. Otherwise, it's like calling yourself an abstract painter because you cannot paint something that is real."

— SYDNEY POLLACK, DIRECTOR

In 1989, aged 11, my life changed when my father bought a family video camera, a big beast of a thing called a "Betamovie," to film family holidays, sports days, that sort of thing . . . but I saw only one real purpose.

I grew up on '70s and '80s adventure movies like *Star Wars*, *Raiders of the Lost Ark*, and *E.T.* I couldn't articulate just how they made me feel: I was buzzing, excitable, and had a rush every time I saw the posters or logos on sticker books and toys. All I knew was that I wanted to be part of that world. When *Indiana Jones and the Last Crusade* was released in 1989, I spent all my pocket money on related books and magazines. I couldn't take my eyes off the stunning photographs from the film contained in those pages. I didn't know what it was about them that I liked, but I was mesmerized. Looking back now I realize it was Douglas Slocombe's gorgeous lighting, the diffusion, the amber backlight, the smoke . . .

One Sunday afternoon, myself, my siblings, and some friends decided to make our own adventure movie. What could be simpler? I knew how I wanted it to look, thanks to Slocombe, and I knew what had to happen — I had the film magazines and I knew Indiana Jones inside and out. But when we watched it back, it was all shot from the same angle, with all the mistakes we made still on the tape: sometimes the sun was out, sometimes it wasn't, and the soundtrack mostly consisted of my neighbor's lawnmower cutting in and out since it was all shot and edited in-camera. Where was John Williams's score? Where was the excitement?

This was when the notions of angles, sound effects, lighting, and editing began to crystalize in my mind.

As the years went on, we made more films, slowly getting more and more adventurous, learning things every step of the way. In the early years I copied shots that I saw in films I liked. They were good shots, but I didn't realize that shots work in a Steven Spielberg or Ridley Scott movie because they fit the emotion of the scene; they might not work cut and pasted into my film. So I learned the first time, as everyone does, by copying others; gradually I changed and added my own takes on things, finding my voice.

A lot of the early stuff I shot by instinct. "Let's put the camera here as it looks good." They were good shots, but what I didn't know was *why* they were good. It was a good shot because it was a wide shot, and told the audience exactly where everything and everyone was. Then I discovered the notions of coverage, and filming a wide shot before some close-ups, and things became a little technical and clinical. Coverage is a good thing but I followed it too rigorously and forgot to be inventive and dynamic. I felt I lost some of the spark in the films I was making. Then the pendulum thankfully swung back the other way, and now I mix instinct and technical ability.

Throughout the short films I produced, I explored different areas of the business: Writing and working with other writers, casting actors and rehearsing, shooting with special effects and pyrotechnics, visual effects, using grip and dolly gear, cranes, different camera formats, editing, having a professional sound mix, working with composers, and finally compliance with delivery and transmission requirements for broadcast. Each area taught me something, and bit by bit I got the experience and knowledge to inform the other disciplines. The amateur films and approaches slowly turned professional; now I do what I love for a living.

Ten years ago, in between filming assignments, colleges and universities around the country asked me to share my film knowledge and experience with young filmmakers. When working with new students, I found that their grasp of theory and technical knowhow didn't always translate into practical application. I wanted to teach the fundamentals and add in a wealth of experience and techniques learned over twenty years freelancing behind the camera. Practical teaching meets theory meets technical information, with a healthy dose of on-set reality.

I like reading about stuff I can use *practically*. Tools, hands-on techniques, and approaches to shooting good images — and fast. After working with a lot of film students, I found there wasn't really a book that listed everything I thought they should learn, so I decided to write it. My former students have become feature-film directors, BBC editors, and successful freelancers in their own right.

Some of the ideas, tools, or techniques might not work for you. Be a "student," not a "follower." Some film books deal with lighting or scriptwriting or the like and mention things I don't really agree with, but the other 95% of the information is pure gold; this book should be treated the same way. Early students sometimes make the mistake of adopting "rules" hard and fast. *"You should never film that way . . ." "You can't use a close-up more than three times or it becomes redundant . . ." "My lecturer says you should never cut from this to that . . ."* I frequently remind my students that there are no absolutes, no rules. My guidelines work and have consistently worked, but if you find an exception and want to do something differently, do it. But make sure what you do comes from a place of personal preference and not what you've heard others say.

Experience and conversation reveal a psychology and a philosophy of filmmaking. There is an aspect of this in any creative art form, whether it is writing, fashion, music, painting, or something else. Psychology is at least 50% of what you are doing; the balance is technical ability — in terms of your work, but moreover your approach and mindset toward it. Confidence, insecurity, doubt, overcompensation, and dealing with incidents and politics on set. These issues never go away. Whatever role you find yourself in, lack of confidence can be stemmed by preparation. If you know you've done all you can and put in the time, you can at least temper your lack of confidence. Or this will help you after the fact, when you know you did all your homework. If you're prepared, then you are a little more relaxed and able to react and think clearly should an incident arise.

After all these years working with students and following them through work or film school, I can now spot the patterns. My first impressions of their abilities and commitment accurately predict where students are now. Those that worked had a positive, productive mindset; those that didn't avoided taking notes in class and reading the books, doing only what they were told to do, nothing more. The ones who lacked that *drive*. You can find out a lot about someone else's philosophy and attitude from their reactions. When you say, "We're shooting in London at 6 am Saturday," and they say, "Yes, see you there," you learn something about their philosophy. If they say, "Does it have to be that early? How far?" you know how they really feel about it. So what would *your* reaction be?

Reading and knowledge are the beginning of things. Knowledge and theory are useless to you unless you put them into *action* so that knowledge finds its value. You need to take action to put everything you learn into practice. Unless you take action on that advice, it is as valuable to you as if you hadn't read it in the first place. So, who do you know? Who can you call? You must TAKE ACTION on what you read. I have tried to impart all the information, experiences, and advice I can remember in each of the chapters. It is up to you to take that information and put it to use. Good luck!

SCENE HEADING
↓   SCENE DE
OURT BUILDING CORRIDOR - DAY
ht filters down the empty dim corr:
ty down the hall, just about reach
r opens and suits and uniforms pile
        early 40s, tall, calm, s
                  looks like

CHAPTER 1

Scriptwriting

"The final cut of the movie is the last draft of the script."
— Quentin Tarantino, writer / director

The script. The screenplay. Also known to some as the blueprint. Everything starts with those pages. It's what gets the interest, the star, the finance, and it's what tells the story. If it's not in the script, it's not on the screen. If anyone tells you after reading their script that a lot of it will come across in how the film is shot, roll it up and bash them over the head with it. I've personally made this mistake and on reflection, you tell yourself that stuff to gloss over the cracks or disguise poor writing. Writing is hard. Some writers love it, some hate it. I find the best thing about writing is having written . . .

So in this chapter I'm going to look at writing the script for your film. It might be for a short film or a feature-length script. You might be writing it to make the film yourself, or for someone else to, as you enjoy the craft and process of writing.

MY START

When I was a teenager making short films with my friends, we all just wanted to be actors in our own movie. But we had to write it first. They were handwritten scripts about 6 pages long — but we thought that would equate to a big feature film. We also realized that just because we've written it and can picture it in our heads doesn't mean we have the resources to get that vision on film. Even today,

I read low-budget student scripts with lines like "the four police cars come to a screeching halt outside the burning house" and the producer in me immediately thinks, "How are you going to film that with your $625 (£500) budget?"

Once I moved to writing features, I took a new approach to the craft. Writing a much bigger story in a longer form meant I had to have the discipline to finish and go a little more in depth with my story and characters. The first few scripts we shot ourselves; then there were a lot of scripts that got written but never saw the light of day. These were still great experiences and homework: working on my craft, finessing my skills, learning to be a better writer.

SHORT VERSUS FEATURE?

Are you writing a short or feature film? Short film scripts are different from feature scripts in ways other than length, but they share a lot of the same elements. There's no harm in having a beginning, middle, and end in a short film script, as well as ideas about form, character, and style. The layout and format are certainly the same. In short films you have the opportunity to play a lot more with structure than you do in a feature. You could write a narrative-based film about a character trying to achieve something with a traditional three-act structure, or it could be a quirky, ambiguous film with an open ending. Some short films end with a twist, while others are basically shortened versions of a feature film.

A film can be any length you choose, but a short film is traditionally about 15 minutes or less. With a page of the script equaling roughly a minute of screen time, a 12–14 page script might give you a 15-minute film. Some film festivals actually accept shorts of any length; others cap them at 40 minutes.

A good length for a feature film script is 90–120 pages. Anything over 120 pages would yield a running time of over two hours.

STORY

What story are you trying to tell? I personally like to find that emotional hook, something that has heart and where I can see how any events or obstacles will affect that. That normally is my "in" to the story.

What's the theme of the story? Is it love, family, jealousy, revenge, fate, destiny, loss? Most times with my work I discover the theme after I've written something. I have themes recur over and over again through the different stories I make. In most cases, this theme turns out to be loss. I tend to gravitate toward that theme more than others.

Starting late in the story is always a good idea. When does your story really get going? Think about the way you tell stories to your friends. When telling the story of how you ran out of gas on the way home from your vacation last week, you don't start with buying the car three years ago. No, you start with what happened just before the car stopped. Anything else is boring to the listener and has no impact on the story. Also start each scene as late as you possibly can in the story. Ask yourself: When do the story and the scene really start?

Whatever your story, it will probably involve the protagonist(s) or hero(es) looking to achieve something or go somewhere to change their current situation. What makes stories interesting is the conflict: obstacles arising on the journey that prevent the subjects from getting what they want. It could be a man wanting to spend the rest of his life with the woman he loves, but the obstacles of distance, marriage, fear, or relatives prevent him from doing so. It could be a hero cop trying to stop a group of villains from robbing and taking over a building and finding themselves subjected to gunfire and explosives. There are literally thousands of possibilities, but it all comes down to those simple fundamentals. If your story is about the character wanting something and they sit still until someone delivers it to them without any fuss, the audience won't be very entertained.

What the audience wants is drama, and all drama is conflict, whether external (physical) or internal (emotional). Having internal conflict that builds to external conflict is good. And on the flipside, external conflict should cause internal conflict. Having more conflict means that there's more stuff for the character(s) to overcome. This gives you material for scenes, and allows for things to get set up that must be resolved by the end of the story. Maybe one conflict / resolution affects another?

RESOLUTIONS

The conclusion to your story is always a hard one. You have to tie up most if not all of the things you have set up during the story and (and here's where the good writing comes in) do it in a way that is satisfactory to the audience. If we have Spider-Man fighting the Green Goblin and we know by the end of the film Spider-Man has to defeat the villain, we want to see that — and it has to be at the hands of the hero. If it ended with Spider-Man watching TV where it's reported that the Green Goblin accidentally got run over by a taxi instead, that wouldn't be satisfactory to the audience. The outcome is the same, but he wasn't defeated by the hero, which is what we want to see.

It's worth noting that resolution doesn't necessarily mean a happy ending. You can resolve the story and have a sad or melancholy conclusion to the events. What sometimes makes a good story is when a character goes out to get something that they need, but by the conclusion of the story gets what they want instead. There is a difference between a want and a need. They need to find the hidden treasure, but end up getting a closer family relationship. They need to win that big contest they've traveled halfway around the world for, but end up getting the girl. In order for the audience to leave the cinema satisfactorily, they need to know that whatever has happened, the character is okay. Whether this is a new perspective on life, or a coming-to-terms with what has happened, or some other sort of conclusion.

STRUCTURE

The structure of your screenplay is perhaps one of the most important aspects. For me, structure is akin to a steel rod down the back of a beautiful clay sculpture. It is never seen or touched by the viewer, but without it the piece would fall to the floor.

Traditionally, we have three-act plays. Three is a nice dramatic number: we are able to tell a story with a beginning, a middle, and an end. Some films in Hollywood have worked off this formula for years. I think it's important to be aware of how films can be structured in order to go off and do your own thing, if that's where you want to go. You could also have two acts, or five. It all depends on the story you're telling.

Make no bones about it: structure is a killer. It's the part of the process where most of the hard work is done, and it can be brutal. As I block out the scenes, I'm aware of how each one affects the tone, the pace, and what information is released to the audience and when. Things need to unfold at just the right time to have maximum effect. It's a jigsaw puzzle of massive proportions.

The first form of traditional structure I was introduced to was the "Hero's Journey," through Christopher Vogler's book *The Writer's Journey: Mythic Structure for Writers*. Vogler's book is itself based on Joseph Campbell's monomyth and *The Hero With a Thousand Faces*.

Elements of the Hero's Journey structure can be found in pretty much all genres: comedies, thrillers, dramas, and horror films. Elements seldom appear in the same order, but they are there to be found, and some films adhere to the sequence more than others. Adventure films such as *Indiana Jones*, *Star Wars*, *Harry Potter*, *Back to the Future*, and *Lord of the Rings* stick very closely to it, as they are literally about a hero's journey, whereas others come and go, touching on some points and ignoring others. You don't have to use this, or adhere to it, but story structure matters. It has been very useful to me over the years.

So what exactly is The Hero's Journey? It's a 12-point list of events that take the story from the beginning to the end, charting the character arc and creating our hero. Let's take a look.

1. **Ordinary World:** This is when we see our hero in their natural environment. Their everyday life. We need to see this to establish a baseline of events before the upcoming change. This is Frodo in the Shire, the cop finishing up an old case, the lonely girl's boring day-to-day life before meeting the mysterious stranger.

2. **Call to Adventure:** This is when our hero gets asked to complete a task, go on an adventure, take a new job, move out of his or her comfort zone,

solve a murder case, or join a team. A problem presents itself that the hero must solve.

3. **Refusal of the Call:** Our hero will always refuse the call in its first instance. They don't feel they're up to the task, they lack confidence, and they'll make any excuse they can find to try and get out of it. A cop refuses the case since he's about to retire, the protagonist refuses to work for the government, etc. Frodo, Indiana Jones, and Luke Skywalker all refuse. Why refuse? Well, not only does the character not feel up to the challenge, diving headfirst into the call will belie their subsequent claims that they didn't want to be there in the first place! The audience can't be thinking, "Well, you asked for this . . ."

4. **Meeting With the Mentor:** Our hero now meets someone who will guide them through their journey. A spiritual guide of sorts who knows the lay of the land and can answer any questions our hero might have. It's Gandalf, Obi-Wan Kenobi, the father figure. Normally associated with step 8 . . . but we'll get to that. This marks the end of Act 1.

5. **Crossing the First Threshold:** This is the start of Act 2, when the story changes direction and the real adventure begins. The hero literally crosses over the threshold from their ordinary world into uncharted territory.

6. **Tests, Allies, Enemies:** Our hero meets the faces inhabiting this new world, a place that tests him or her. The hero's new friends will help complete the task and confront the villain.

7. **Approach the Inmost Cave:** The hero has to come face to face with the enemy or something unknown. They're entering the dragon's lair, the dark cave where we don't know what lies ahead. They must summon the courage to go to this place, physically, mentally, or both. They doubt their abilities, and must use skills they've always had but didn't know they possessed.

8. **The Supreme Ordeal:** What is the worst thing that can happen to our hero, apart from death? That is the supreme ordeal. In most cases, the guiding light of the mentor that has gotten them this far is taken from them. A companion dies, they lose the funding, they lose the job, all is lost. This is where the heart of the film lies, what the whole film is about. This marks the end of Act 2.

9. **Reward:** The hero survives the battle with the enemy and is transformed into a new person. It is here they find the reward or item they have sought on their journey, whether it is physical or a new insight.

10. **The Road Back:** They escape the new world, heading home, most probably defined by some sort of chase or escape. This is the time to show the new skills they have learned on the quest.

11. **Resurrection or Rebirth:** Maybe the villain isn't quite dead yet and things aren't quite finished for the hero. Here they're reborn as the people they have always wanted to be.

12. **Return with Elixir:** The hero returns to the old world and hands the Elixir to the people that requested it, curing the original problem. Anything left unanswered will be answered here. The journey is complete.

So, as mentioned, some or all of these elements are found in 99% of stories. Ordinary World, Call to Adventure, and Refusal of the Call come at the start of most films, whatever the genre. The romantic comedies, the thrillers, the dramas. This is all good character stuff, an opportunity to see a character before things change, and witness their outlook and life philosophy.

Even short films can feature some of these elements. You don't have the running time to play with all of them, but some of these elements can be found in shorter films and they can make the characters and story stronger for it.

FORMATTING

There are different script-formatting templates depending on what type of show you are making, whether it is a film screenplay, TV sitcom, stage play, or radio program. If you want to write a sitcom for the BBC, for example, they have a preferred format. For our purposes, I'll concentrate on a film script (feature or short). All the elements of story, character, dialogue, etc., will be relevant, whatever format you're writing for. However, these are industry guidelines, not rules. People break these guidelines all the time as their material and styles dictate. However, if 99% of the industry understands something to work best a certain way, there's no harm in doing the same. Just to highlight the point that there are no "rules," a literary agent who represents many new writers once told me that while she considered formatting important, she'd once received a handwritten script with none of the layout rules followed, but with writing that was so good and funny that she took the new writer on. The official formatting of scripts can be taught or learned later, but the talent here was in the writing.

The standard typeface is Courier, font size 12. There is also no bold highlighting in the scene headings or scene descriptions. No underlining or any fancy special character graphics your computer can produce. I'd also suggest not doubling spaces between paragraphs or using a larger size font or any other tricks to up the page count. It doesn't look good, and ultimately could be tricking you and the crew into thinking there is more to shoot or plan than necessary.

A scene in your script has four elements to it:
- Scene heading or slug line
- Scene description / action
- Character name
- Dialogue

Scene headings, sometimes called a slug line, are displayed as follows:

`INT/EXT. WAREHOUSE — NIGHT`

Scene headings are all in capitals, and the INT. tells the reader whether we are inside (interior) or outside (EXT. for exterior). Then we see what time of day it is: DAY, NIGHT, DUSK, SUNRISE. If we change the story's time or place, we change the scene heading. If we move from one side of the room to another, we don't need a new heading. But if characters move outside, or we stay in the same location but time passes, we need a new scene heading since production will treat it as a new scene. One script I reviewed was set at a single location and time of day but somehow warranted six different scene headings! The writer, it turned out, had confused "scene headings" with "camera shots."

When a character speaks, their name is in CAPITALS with the dialogue underneath. If a character speaks in a foreign language, write in English or your chosen language and use parentheticals, i.e., *(in French)* to tell the reader. The abbreviation (O.S.) is used to let the reader know that what is being said by a character is OFFSCREEN. We can hear them, but we can't see them.

Take a look at this sample script page to see how it all comes together.

```
                    ┌─────────────────┐
FADE IN               SCENE HEADING
                    └─────────────────┘
                             ↓            ┌──────────────────────────────┐
                                            SCENE DESCRIPTION/ACTION
                                          └──────────────────────────────┘
INT. COURT BUILDING CORRIDOR - DAY                    ↓

Daylight filters down the empty dim corridor. Echoes of
activity down the hall, just about reach us.

A door opens and suits and uniforms pile out. Among them,
MICHAEL CHAPEL, early 40s, tall, calm, sombre. Michael and
his lawyer, LAWRENCE, 40, but looks like he just graduated,
step out of the river of officials leaving the court. The
medals on Michael's Army uniform catch the fading light.

                    LAWRENCE  ←─────────  ┌───────────┐
             I think this calls for a couple of  CHARACTER
             Glenfiddichs, on me.             └───────────┘

His elation isn't shared by Michael.

                    LAWRENCE (CONT'D)
             Well, it's a good job your
             conscience wasn't on that Court  ←──  ┌──────────┐
             Marshall, Michael, or I would have      DIALOGUE
             broken my winning streak.             └──────────┘

Michael finds a nearby bench, undoes his top button, followed
by a deep exhale of breath.

Lawrence's question catches up with him.

                    MICHAEL
             Sorry Lawrence.  Still processing.
             (considers it for moment) No, sorry
             I have to go back to work.

Lawrence takes his cue.

                    LAWRENCE
             Well, give me a call next week and
             we can go over and sign what's left
             to complete.

Michael still deep in thought, doesn't see Lawrence pass a
WOMAN and her HUSBAND quickly approaching. The woman, 60s
slows to meet Michael's bench. He catches her presence and
stands respectfully.

She slaps him across the face. Hard.  Tears in her eyes.

                    WOMAN
             We won't forget our son.  And
             neither should you.
```

1.1 Sample script page

SCENE DESCRIPTIONS / ACTION

This is when your writing really shines, or you make it really hard for the reader by doing a substandard job. The descriptions or action tell us what is happening in the scene. It also tells about important objects, and what the characters are doing. You tell this story by creating pictures in the audience's mind — these are motion pictures, not radio. Try to describe not how something *looks*, but how it *feels*. Describe any motion occurring, not still objects or characters. Once we know where we are, thanks to the scene heading, what's important is what happens. It is also acceptable to use fragmented sentences when writing action. It makes things a bit easier to read, and keeps the pace swift.

You are only looking to describe what is seen, heard, or moves. You can't describe what a character feels or thinks; this isn't a novel. Writing "John remembers that the girl in the picture was the same girl he met at the party last year" cannot be displayed on screen; the camera cannot show it to the audience. The reader would then have information that the viewer doesn't. This is called "embedded information." Sometimes you see a solitary character say to themselves, "Oh God, that's the girl from the party last year . . ." Bad writing comes in many forms, like this approach. Try to find a visual way to give the audience the information it needs.

POETRY

Something I learned late in the game was to be a little more poetic with my descriptions. The feeling I wanted to convey was in my head, but the descriptions I'd write were fairly standard and pedestrian. Reading my words induced the desired feeling, but my language fell short. When others read my work, they didn't feel it the same way I did. It didn't translate. A writer friend had a story about an extroverted, party-going thirtysomething. Her scene started with the woman hung over from a heavy night on the town. Her scene description read:

```
INT. EMMA'S BEDROOM — DAY

It is the morning after the night before.
```

What can we conclude from this? I would guess that Emma is asleep but still dressed, sprawled over the bed, one leg hanging off the edge, hair and makeup a mess, bottles everywhere. You want the descriptions to be fun to read, but not too cutesy or ostentatious. Style is one thing, but trying too hard to be different or entertaining is unappealing in the same way as fancy lighting or jazzy editing might be. Lighting and editing are at their best when they are invisible; they have the desired effect, but don't draw attention to themselves. It is the same with writing.

CHARACTER'S ACTIONS

Most characters "walk" places or "look" at things. That is one way to describe their actions, I suppose. Have a think about what they are *really* doing. Are they "glancing," "staring," "ogling"? Maybe they're not walking or running, but "strutting," "jogging," "sauntering"? These descriptions help build a clearer picture, and most importantly reflect character as well as action.

If you want to emphasize something, you could use capital letters. The car SMASHES into the building and then EXPLODES into a fireball. Again, use caps sparingly, or you might dilute impact.

CHARACTERS

What do your characters WANT? Nothing else matters. Actors may benefit from talking about what their character had for breakfast or intricate details of props or costumes, but what really matters (and is sometimes forgotten) is what their character "wants." That's it. That's the story.

Dramatic need is another way of talking about a character's want. Once decided, it then becomes a matter of what obstacles can be placed in their way to prevent them from achieving this. If they achieve their need, a new need immediately replaces it. If this isn't set up early, the story can't really begin. We can't identify with the hero's struggle until we know what that struggle is and why they are faced with it.

The protagonist's entrance is always exciting for me to write. We need to know when the hero or heroine just walked on the stage. Write for the star, and look after the star at all times. We need a physical description, but also an extra element of their personality and inner character. What description can you think of in a couple of lines that can create a picture of that character in the reader's mind?

```
Sarah, tall, confident, larger than life, 40s but
going on 21.
```

What could be assumed of her actions? How she holds herself? How she dresses?

So it's not just the description you need to think about, but also their actions. What's the first thing we see them do? The best way to convey character is through action. Is there something they can do physically, or better yet visually, that shows us who they really are? Even in our everyday lives, if you want to understand who a person is, look at what they *do*, not what they *say*.

BACKSTORY

Your character's backstory is what has happened to the character before the script began. What has happened to them from when they were born to page one of the script? You don't need to write or know their complete history, but you do need to know anything relevant to the story. Is there something bad that still haunts them, keeps them up at night? Did they make a mistake in a job or relationship that they still need to rectify? Does everyone know their history, or is it a secret? Each of the main three characters in Steven Spielberg's *Jaws* (1975) has a backstory shaped by water. Al Pacino's character in *Scent of a Woman* (1992) is blind, bitter, and angry, and we later find out he was in the army and had an accident juggling live grenades! The opening of Alfred Hitchcock's *Rear Window* (1954) introduces the main character in its opening frames AND gives us his backstory at the same time. We see Jimmy Stewart sitting in a wheelchair looking out the rear window of his apartment with his leg in a cast. The camera pans around the room and we see a broken camera alongside pictures of race cars crashing and flying around the track. So we now know who he is and what happened to him. Total lines of dialogue spoken: zero.

DIALOGUE

Dialogue is the fun part, but can also be very hard to write. What do people say to each other? Most dialogue is not needed and is overwritten. Leading actors are famous for taking lines out of the script, not for adding more. They want to be the people that know the information, not the ones who are going around asking questions. The dialogue has to ring true for the character and situation, so dialogue is driven by what the characters want. Once you know who the character is and their backstory, and actively consider their identity while crafting dialogue, you will know what the character should be saying.

Most scenes (and scripts) work best if you cut the top and the bottom off. We usually like to embellish a little at either end when we simply don't need it. People walk into rooms, have small talk, then talk about what's important and leave the room with the good stuff in the middle. Certainly if someone storming out of the room to leave another party in solitary reflection is part of the story, then keep it, but the dialogue in the middle is the heart.

Parentheticals, or ( ), tell the reader of any additional action or details of the character's attitude. They appear directly under the character's name and before or during the dialogue. Try to not use too many, though. How someone is talking should be evident from the scene. If you need to stress "angry" or "sarcastic" then do it, but not above every line. You can also use parentheticals for small elements of stage directions like "puts paper down" or "closes eyes." A nice tool to help make things clear, but only use it when you need to.

PLANTS AND PAYOFFS

A plant is an object, event, line, or action that is put in the script very early on that is then called upon to help save the day or cause an issue later in the story. We've seen it all before: an insignificant character who has a certain skill, or the detective who keeps a gun under the table, or those sharp, dangerous objects unearthed in the hero's house when decorating. Hope the villain doesn't fall on them when he bursts in to the hero's house at the end. The trick here is to plant this object, line, or action as early as you can in the story, just enough for the audience to forget about it. When it comes up again later to save the day, it is a surprise to them and they didn't jump ahead and see it coming. If you plant it late and pay it off a few scenes later, it might come across as a terrible coincidence, and you risk losing your audience.

A good way to work this plant / payoff idea into your script is to find out what you might need at the end of your story, then reverse-engineer it by sprinkling the objects / setups throughout the beginning and middle of your script. An example of this is from the James Bond film *Goldeneye* (1995). Early on in the film, Bond is given an array of gadgets by Q, one of which is an exploding pen that is activated once clicked three times. Later on, Bond finds himself held hostage next to a fidgety computer hacker who just happens to be using Bond's pen. Explosions ensue . . .

1.2 *Goldeneye*

REWRITING

It's tough getting to the end of your script. Endings need a lot of work, but seeing that last page coming at you like light at the end of a tunnel is exciting. The rewrite is where the real work is done, so be ready. You want to transform it from a stack of bound-together pages to something that sparkles and that people can't put down.

Most work is 25% better if it's 25% shorter. That goes for everything: movies, essays, scripts, books . . . On the first pass of the script, you almost certainly indulged in overly detailed scene descriptions, people spoke to each other for too long, and five or six unnecessary scenes remained. We all do it. Go over each of your scenes and find what is the latest possible point that you can come into them so that they still makes sense. What happens if you chop off the start and the end? What you're left with will probably be better.

Go through and adjust. Can the scene description be more poetic? Can you add a sprinkle of character to the action? Will the audience assume certain things so they needn't be described or shown? Read the script from the audience's point of view. Whenever we subsequently view the film, we watch knowing what we know and seeing everything through those glasses. When I'm writing or editing, I literally stop the edit or hold the page to ask, "Do we know where we are and what this person is doing?" "Is it clear what is happening here?" You know as the writer where the characters are going, but do we as the reader?

Now get writing!

CHAPTER 2

Producing

"You need to be willing to take the heat . . . You need to take responsibility for your actions in business."

— DAWN STEEL, PRODUCER / STUDIO EXECUTIVE

Producers: the backbone of any project. They hire and they fire. They run the show. Their job is to provide everything they can to the director, and give the production what it needs to get the job done. Producers are the bosses. A good way to describe a producer is:

They're the first person on a project and the last one to leave.

THE DIFFERENT TYPES OF PRODUCERS

There are various types of producers. We have the following:

Producer — Highest-ranking person involved on a project. They collect the Oscar when Best Picture is announced.

Executive Producer — This credit is normally given to someone who got a project going and started its development, but then handed it over to the producer. They also could be a financial investor in the film who never sets foot on set.

Co-Producer — This role might involve taking on a little bit of the work from the producer and someone who performs a key role in the film (but answers to the producer).

Associate Producer — A junior producer who might take on some of the functions of the producer, but like the co-producer still answers to the producer.
Line Producer — This is normally a role dealing with the film budget. Sometimes the line producer's duties come under the title "production coordinator."

This book focuses on the role of the producer. For the work you'd be most likely to undertake, the producer role will be an amalgamation of all the above descriptions. I'm also going to mainly concentrate on the actual production aspects of the film. Raising finance, distribution, and selling the end product would cover a whole other book and would be primarily dealt with when producing feature films.

THE STAGES OF PRODUCTION

The production of a film happens in three phases:

Pre-production — *Scripting, castings, location recces, set building, planning, and crewing.*
Production — *The shooting of the film.*
Post-production — *Editing, grading, sound mixing, visual effects, music, marketing, and distribution.*

These are the stages where certain roles or functions are performed, but they can overlap and as a producer you should be thinking about all of them. Even though editing and marketing traditionally take place in the post-production phase, you should be planning and organizing during pre-production. You also need to know your formats and post-production workflow before you begin shooting. You might need to deliver the film on time in order to make a film-festival or tax-break deadline, so having your post workflow established is paramount.

Besides the director, the producer should also have a clear idea of the vision, the tone, and the theme of the film. They are also party to decisions and need to know things to keep the project on track. A film, like any business, is run in the image of its leaders. As the producer or director, you are that leader. If you are organized, pragmatic, and decisive, then the film, its operation, and the set floor will reflect this.

MY START

When my friends and I started making short films, producing was something we did automatically without realizing we were doing it. If we wanted to make our own films, we had to organize and arrange their production — simple stuff like deciding when we could film and where, who would be in the production, what props we needed, and who was going to pay for the rental or purchase of that particular prop. Respect, manners, and professionalism all come into play here and were all learnt in these early days. Some people still haven't found these skills yet, even as adults! As a producer shooting small student films, I had to find ways to achieve what I wanted and think a little more laterally and outside the box, like the time when I needed a helicopter to take off for the finale of a particular project. At $565 (£450) an hour to rent, it was my complete budget back in 1996, but I suggested we film our cast climbing on board just before the helicopter company had an actual booking, and then I shot them and their client taking off. Editing did the rest.

APPLYING THE BASICS:

HOW DO YOU BECOME A "PRODUCER"?

So what do we have to think about when we produce? The script, camera / lighting equipment, actors, locations, permissions, food, travel / accommodation, post-production, marketing, insurance, budget, scheduling, health and safety, contracts . . . the list goes on, but let's look at a few.

BUDGET

First and foremost, before anything is booked or planned you need to know your budget. This is perhaps the biggest thing the producer has to be on top of. How much is this thing going to cost? Can it be done for the budget allotted? Maybe the project is self-funded, in which case, do YOU have enough money? Either way, money is the number-one issue. You cut your coat to suit the cloth. The budget and scheduling go hand in hand; one affects the other. You want more days to shoot, then it'll cost more. More of everything: crew, food, accommodation, gear rental . . . but let's look at what goes in the budget first, then examine scheduling.

BUDGETING FOR CREW

The crew list for a corporate video might be significantly smaller than what is required for a drama. On a corporate, you might have a person on camera, sound, and maybe a producer or director. For a drama, the camera department might consist of a director of photography, camera operator, 1st camera assistant (focus puller), and 2nd camera assistant (clapper / loader). For each of these projects you might have to tweak the crew accordingly. Every crew member is important, but sometimes the budget will make the decisions for you. You'll find yourself asking: "Can the actors do their own make-up?" "Can the camera operator also manage the sound?" "Could the producer be the grip?" The areas in which you're cutting back on crew can and will have an effect on production. Yes, in a coffee-shop drama, the actors could do their own make-up; but in the zombie film, you can't afford to cut the make-up team from the budget! As the producer it is your job to make these decisions. Sometimes it's hard to cut people out or say no to them. If every department got what they wanted, this would add more time and more money. Then you'd be out of a job, and so would they.

BUDGETING FOR GEAR RENTAL

One decision that will have a large knock-on effect on many other departments is what camera you shoot on. The director of photography and the director will have a discussion with the producer and decide what format best suits the project at hand. If you are all these people, then that decision is yours.

What lights are required is also a large budgetary consideration. Ask the director of photography for their lighting-gear list. This will almost always be quite a large wish list that will have to be cut down. Ask the lighting-rental company what arrangements can be made. Transportation of this camera and lighting gear will also have to factor into your budget. Maybe the rental company can supply a small van, or you might have to pursue a separate, external van rental. Then ask yourself: Which crew member is happy to drive it? Maybe the project size means that the small lighting units can all fit in the trunk of your car? Just make sure to check with your insurance company that it is all covered.

BUDGETING FOR FOOD / TRAVEL / ACCOMMODATION

Depending on where your shoot takes place, you may be looking at having to transport your cast and crew to locations miles from your home base. This would mean sorting their travel, putting them up in local accommodation, and feeding them. This can really put a hole in your budget if you're not careful. If people are working for next to nothing or exactly nothing, the least you can do is feed them and feed them well. Pizzas every night will simply not suffice either!

So the questions to ask are: How much are you going to spend on each person per head and over how many days? What food will you be buying and from where? Are the cast and crew all staying in hotels or bed and breakfasts? Who will require travel costs? Will it be a train, bus, or taxi? If they're driving themselves, are gas costs being covered, and at what rate? At a base cost, or at 55 cents (45 pence) a mile?

SCHEDULE

Does the project have to be delivered by a certain time? This will affect your choices on settings, crews, and cameras. If the answer is yes, then work back from that date.

After producing a few short films you start to get a feel of how long things take to shoot. A short drama with minimal locations and a running time of anywhere between 20–30 minutes might take roughly four days to shoot. If this short film had numerous exterior night scenes involving lots of extras and visual effects, this might grow to 6–8 days. In the past I've not scheduled enough time, thinking, "Oh, it's only a small scene, we can bang that out in a couple of hours . . ." But you fail to allow for the late arrivals, the setup time, the technical issues that come up, and any discussions with actors . . .

For shoots involving lots of extras / supporting actors, visual effects, or exciting bits of grip equipment, schedule double or triple the amount of time you think scenes might take, as these elements will always slow your shooting day down. Problems arise, like time issues from resetting background artists for another take, and rigging that nice, expensive hothead crane! They all add up.

PAPERWORK, RECEIPTS, AND MONEY

It is your responsibility to manage the books. Balancing the checkbook and making sure the creditors aren't calling are part of your job. A good producer has excellent organizational skills too, and is able to put their hands on any document or piece of information at a moment's notice. The amount of paperwork that even a small production can incur is surprising. Extras must sign release forms, location owners need permissions, and there may be plentiful contracts with distribution companies or TV stations. Keep all email correspondence too as it's legally binding.

There is a money trail when you rent gear, pay for insurance, and settle invoices with your crew. Here's a good tip, and it puzzles me why it's not a more popular one: If the money is in the bank and you have the cash available, pay the rental companies, the crews, *everyone* straight away. It's very good business practice. A month's worth of negligible interest on your payroll is small reward in light of the massive amount of benefits, goodwill, and personal favors you may earn for the remainder of the shoot (and onto the next one) for paying promptly. Next time you rent from the camera-equipment company, they'll remember you paid quickly, so it's in their best interest to look after you. Besides, it's a job done! You don't have to worry about still making payment, or worse, receiving that email "reminding" you you're overdue. I've had those, and believe me, it's not a nice feeling.

Keep all your receipts and invoices so there are records of everything. Every time you purchase stationery or camera cards or even pay for drinks at that production meeting, the receipt gets kept and stored away safely.

CALL SHEETS

A "call sheet" is a document every member of the cast and crew gets issued every day of a shoot. It has all the important and relevant information on it: the day, location, and contact information; what's being filmed, who is involved, and what the call times are; and any other details you require. It also lists where the nearest hospital is in the event of an accident, what time the sun sets at the location, and who is responsible for bringing any pieces of specialized gear. Some even have an advanced schedule of what is being planned for the following few days' shooting. On the following page you can find a call sheet example with the main information listed.

In the table listing what is being filmed that day, the column titled "page" refers to the amount of the script that particular scene involves. A script is broken into 1/8ths of a page, so if a scene took up half a page, it would be listed on the call sheet as 4/8ths of a page. A single line of stage directions might only be 1/8. Filming on any given day could vary between multiple scenes shot at various locations, all lasting an eighth of a page, or just one scene in one location lasting four and three-eighths of a page. D/N refers to whether the scene is set during the day or at night.

HANOVER PICTURES

"We May Be Shadows"

CALL SHEET #1   SHOOT DAY: 1 of 3

DIRECTOR Paul Dudbridge	**DATE :** Saturday 9th January 2010
PRODUCERS Paul Dudbridge	**WEATHER:** Chance of rain 45%
DOP Roger Pearce	**UNIT CALL :** 8am **WRAP :** 7pm **approx**
1st **AD** David Canelo	**SUNRISE: 08.12 SUNSET: 16.22**

Location 1:

Vision Studios Old Mill Road Portishead Bristol, BS20 7BX	Parking: On site.

SCENE	SYNOPSIS	D/N	PAGE	CAST ID	LOCATION
1	INT. BEDROOM: Ed moves to bathroom/comes back	N	3 4/8	1,2	1
1B	INT. BATHROOM: Ed splashes cold water on his face	N	4/8	1	1
1C	INT. LIVING ROOM: Ed sits on sofa, head in hands	N	2/8	1	1
1D	INT. HALLWAY: Ed leaves flat	N	2/8	1	1
4	EXT. NOWHERELAND: GREENSCREEN Ed opens his eyes	N	1	1	1
		TOTAL PAGES	5 4/8		

NO	ARTIST	CHARACTER	TRAVEL	P/UP	CALL	M-UP/HAIR	SET
1	Pete Townsend	Ed Bracken	CAR	07:30:00	08:00:00	08:15:00	08:45:00
2	Margaret Desallais	Alice Bracken	CAR	07:30:00	08:00:00	08:15:00	08:45:00

Notes:
- No filming or photographs to be taken on set please. Unless permission has been given by the Producer. This applies to EVERYONE including visitors.
- Lunch provided. Drinks and snacks available throughout the day.
- FIRST AIDER: Paul Dudbridge

ACCIDENT & EMERGENCY:

Bristol Royal Infirmary tel - 0117 923 0000 Marlborough Street Bristol BS2 8HW	**POLICE:** Trinity Road Police Station tel - 101 Trinity Road St Phillips Bristol BS2 0NW

2.1 Sample call sheet

On a larger-scale film or television drama, the 2nd assistant director will draw up the call sheet, but on smaller-scale projects from short dramas to features with smaller crews, this would fall to the producer. I have a blank template that I can fill in where necessary. I can then export the file as a PDF or Word document and send it out to all the cast and crew. A little tip: Make sure you go over the call sheet with a fine-toothed comb and triple-check all details. There is a lot of important information listed on it, and I've received (and sent out) call sheets with old dates, wrong times, and missing data. This does not reflect well on production. The amount of organization that has to take place before the call sheet can be drawn up is quite immense.

ARRANGING LOCATIONS

When dealing with locations you wish to shoot on, whether owned by a company or privately, there are a few considerations you should take into account. It all starts with your communication. How you first approach them will set the tone and represent the professional level at which you intend to work. It's very easy for people to say no to you. Don't give them a reason to by the manner in which you conduct yourself. I find an email works better than a telephone call; you can plan what you want to say and give all the relevant information needed to make a decision. That email can be forwarded up the management chain of command without having to reiterate the same information to someone else. It also acts as something they can come back and refer to themselves at a later date. Give them the information they need before their imagination takes over, making it as easy as possible for them to say yes.

If you get the all-clear from the person you're dealing with, make sure you ask if there is anyone else in their company that needs to sign off. I've been ambushed by this myself when a day before the shoot my contact has rung to say that they've mentioned it to the boss and received a no. So ask: Who has the authority to sign off on the shoot? In addition, send them a location permission form to get something in writing.

LIMITING THE VARIABLES

Throughout any production of any size you will encounter what I call "variables." Variables are unknown quantities that have the power to hinder or cause problems for the production. Variables could include an unfamiliar new camera, shooting at a higher resolution, using visual effects, working with children or animals, building sets for the first time, shooting underwater, or filming in a strange location. Any situation with which you lack experience can be problematic. The best advice is to limit as many of these variables as possible. The wrong cluster of variables can doom a shoot. For example, maybe you've made a few small short films and a music video, and you're about to embark on your first feature film. Your previous shorts may have been small one-location dramas, but for your feature you embark on a futuristic action film, shooting on a new camera filming at 4K resolution that will feature heavy visual effects, large sets, and child actors. Too many variables!

BEING RESOURCEFUL

When scheduling your location days, be as resourceful as you can and ask what can be shot at the same time. Shooting all of your scenes at a single location, or all of a certain actor's scenes in succession, will save you a great deal of trouble. This of course will require you to be well organized since that last scene at the location might involve a big make-up effect or costume change, the origins of which you haven't shot yet.

Try and be mindful of scale and ambition. Not to hinder or crush big ideas or aspirations, but it is possible to be overly ambitious and not pull off what you intended. This is a sure sign to audiences that they're watching a student / low-budget film! If your script calls for a setting and you don't have the budget or resources to pull it off, think creatively and laterally about another setting that does fulfill what the script calls for but won't look like a pale imitation. It's far better to film at a smaller location or shoot a sequence and have it be the best that it can be than to aim for loftier, more ambitious sights. It is then evident to all you obviously didn't have the resources to make it work. An amazing looking plan B is better than a shoddy, poorly staged plan A. It is here that your film does come off looking cheap. The audience won't remember or know what location you originally had in mind. However, they will notice the cheap staging and the attempt to pull the wool over their eyes when they see that on screen.

THE PERCEPTION OF A PRODUCER

It's also worth noting: Beware of the perception of what a producer is. Some people believe that in order to get stuff done you somehow need to be bullish, hard, rude, and confrontational. I've witnessed this from other producers; it's not very becoming or helpful for the job. Address any serious issues, of course, using a firm, decisive approach as required, but don't make a pre-emptive strike or flex your power to let people know you are in charge. Don't come down hard on people in person, on set, or via email when the situation hasn't reached that threshold yet just because you like the feeling your position gives you. This is poor management and a misuse of the position, whatever industry you're in. I've seen producers make "decisive" decisions without all the facts being available, but they think not acting appears weak. Do not be this person. Adopt and practice the skills of listening, being assertive, being polite, and losing the ego, and it'll make everyone's filming experience a much more enjoyable one.

CHAPTER 3

Camera and Lighting

*"I'd rather see a well-written, well-acted, well-directed but badly
photographed film than a well-photographed but boring film."*
— Peter Suschitzky, cinematographer

Cameras are changing all the time, and at an alarming rate. There was a time that
there were a half-dozen TV and film cameras that were used for production, and
now there's a half-dozen new camera models released each month. It used to be
that the consumer market and the professional market were miles apart; now,
though, student films and low-end promos / TV can be made using the same
cameras as high-end feature films. This new, level playing field further highlights
the importance of what you *do* with the camera — its placement, movement, and
frame composition — as being paramount to *which* camera you use. So before I
discuss cinematography theory and approach, I will go over a few camera basics
to provide a little foundation. This is the biggest chapter in this book, and occa-
sionally it might get a little technical, but bear with me as it's all information you
need to know.

CAMERA BASICS

Most of the basic functions and buttons you can see on a camera are pretty
universal. They might be called by a slightly different name, or be on another part
of the camera body, but they'll be on there somewhere.
- Record button

- Aperture / f-stop
- ISO / Gain / EI
- Shutter
- Focus ring
- Zoom
- Neutral Density (ND) filters
- White balance
- Playback function
- Sound inputs and monitor / output sockets

I have known a lot of students who fall at the first hurdle and think they will never learn camera or lighting, so they put no more effort into trying. On the flipside, I have also been witness to a few "eureka" moments when it really clicks with a student and they're so happy that they now understand things. This sense of growth, learning, and moving forward is really inspiring, and it spreads to other areas. Every cameraperson, even seasoned professionals, has to go through this routine when learning a new camera for a job. So this introduction to finding functions and buttons never really goes away.

To start, turn the camera on. Nothing can follow until we have found the "on" button. Then there will be a button enabling you to switch between recording and playback. They're either labeled "Camera / Media," "Camera / Playback," or have two little icons. This is fairly self-explanatory, enabling you to record and play back your shots.

EXPOSURE

When light travels into your camera through the lens on the front, you need to help the camera make sense of what it is seeing and how much of it to take in. Whatever light you are using, it has an intensity and a color, and this light can be from the sun, which would be considered a natural source, or from film lights you bring to set.

The exposure of your image is controlled by a number of functions. They are the aperture, the ISO, the shutter speed, and the neutral density (ND) filters.

APERTURE / F-STOPS

The aperture controls how much light to let into the camera's sensor to give you an image. Closing down the aperture more will let less light in; opening it up will let more light in. If you film in low light levels, maybe at night or in a dark room, open up your aperture to get a good viewable image. If, however, you film outside in midday sun, close down the aperture to let less light in and prevent the image turning very white and blown out. A good way to think of it is like an iris in your eye. When it gets darker, your iris opens up to let more light into your retina. The camera likely has a button labeled "Iris" or "F-Stop."

3.1 F-stops on the lens

The f-stop is the ratio of the focal length of the lens on your camera to the diameter of your iris or aperture. The focal length is the distance from the sensor in the camera to the focusing element on the lens. If you had a 32mm lens on your camera, and closed the iris or aperture to 8mm in diameter, and we divide 32 by 8, it would equal 4. Our f-stop would be 4. But for what we need to know now, the f-stop is the size of your aperture.

F-stops have values of 1, 1.4, 2, 2.8, 4, 5.6, 8, 11, 16, and 22. There are variations between these numbers, but these are the whole numbers of equal measure apart. When the f-stop number INCREASES, the size of the aperture DECREASES, letting in less light. People tend to think "smaller number, smaller hole," but the opposite is true.

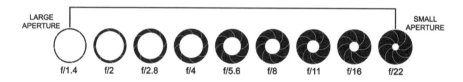

3.2 F-stop diagram

Even though the numbers don't appear to reflect this, each time that the aperture is closed down a full stop — from 2 to 2.8 or from 5.6 to 8, for example — it halves the amount of light coming in. Or, when opening up a full stop, the light being allowed in doubles. Think "smaller number, bigger hole" or "bigger number, smaller hole." Don't get too lost in the math; you just need to know how to use the f-stop to create your images. On most cameras it is controlled by turning the f-stop ring on the lens.

DEPTH OF FIELD

F-stops can also be used to control depth of field. Depth of field refers to the points in your shot that are nearest to and farthest from the camera that look sharp and in focus. If you shoot with a small f-stop, say, f/8, and focus on your subject, your subject and the background will both be in focus. If you wanted more of the background to be out of focus, you would open your aperture to something like f/2.8. Take a look at the images on the next page to see depth of field in action.

3.3 Shallow depth of field

3.4 Large depth of field

When you initially open up your aperture, your image may go a little bright, so you will have to compensate for that by using your camera's neutral density (ND) filters to cut down on the light coming in. We will come to ND filters very shortly.

A good way to remember which f-stop does what is to imagine a row of people standing in front of the camera. At f/2, two people will be in focus. At f/22, twenty-two people will be in focus.

Some camera operators like to shoot what is called "wide open," which is having the smallest f-stop possible, maybe f/1.4 or f/2. This means a lot of the image is out of focus behind your subject and can really help guide the audience as to where to look in the frame. However, there are pros and cons to this approach. If you have a camera assistant whose job it is to focus the camera, it might prove rather difficult (though not impossible) to make sure the actor or subject stays sharp, especially if they are moving! On the flipside, these images do have a very pleasing look, and can make the audience feel like they are watching something a little more "expensive." Having a shallow depth of field, like in the example above, is commonly associated with bigger-budget productions or Hollywood movies. A shallow depth of field can be a wonderful tool to not only make your images look more expensive, but also help the audience with your storytelling. "Pulling focus" (moving the focal point from one object or person to another) shows the audience where to look, and can add a sense of involvement.

With the introduction of new DSLR cameras, it is now common that the depth of field is very shallow due to the camera sensor being very big. But while a single shot with a shallow depth of field taken in isolation might look very good, there is a danger of losing a sense of place within the scene. Lengthy edits of shots with a shallow focus may cause the audience to lose their orientation since they are being deprived of a background for a long period of time. Remember, there is more to photography than a shallow depth of field! However, having a large depth of field is increasingly a big factor in branding the feel and look of low-budget films, making it hard to distinguish itself from the video or TV news look commonly associated with it

ISO / GAIN / EI (EXPOSURE INDEX)

The ISO / Gain / EI refers to how sensitive the camera's sensor is to light. Or, rather, how well the sensor "sees" in low light conditions. Before video cameras, it was based on the sensitivity of the film stock running through the camera. ISO stands for International Standards Organization, and it is a standardized industry scale for measuring sensitivity to light. Most cameras now have an ideal ISO rating.

Upping or lowering the camera's ISO while all of your other camera settings are locked results in the image getting brighter or darker. If you found that in low light conditions you were shooting "wide open" at f/1.8 or f/2 and needing more light, you could up the ISO or gain setting to give you more "light." More light gained through this process will also yield more grain or noise since the image is being artificially boosted to give you a brighter image. Using this method, image quality will slowly deteriorate as images get brighter. Smaller advances in the gain can help you out of low-light difficulties, but know the camera and how far you can push it before your efforts become noticeable. The base ISO of modern cameras is around 850. However, some newer cameras now on the market have a base ISO of 2000!

As with all exposure settings, the trick is to know and understand how they work together. If you found you had some focus problems shooting with a shallow depth of field, you could try upping the ISO to make a brighter image, then closing down your aperture to compensate and achieve the same brightness, but with a bigger depth of field. This way your focus puller or camera operator will have a better chance of keeping the subject sharp.

SHUTTER SPEED

A shutter is essentially a small door between the lens and the camera sensor or film stock that opens and closes very quickly, allowing light through the aperture and exposing the image. The speed at which the shutter or door is open can vary; a quick opening and closing would mean less light coming in.

All modern digital cameras have an electronic shutter, a descendant of film's mechanical shutter that uses the same principles. A shutter helps control your exposure and image by allowing light to enter the camera for a set time. Essentially, it is the amount of time that your sensor "sees" the image in front of it that the camera is trying to capture.

Shutter speeds are measured in fractions of a second. For video and film, the standard shutter speed in the UK is 1/50th of a second and in the US it is 1/48th. Shutter is another factor in controlling your exposure, and works hand in hand with your f-stop and ISO. In 99% of cases you should keep your shutter at 1/50th (or 1/48th), which produces a pleasing look and gives a certain amount of clarity and even blur to moving objects; this is very close to the same way your eye would see the action. Upping your shutter speed to 1/500th of a second would cut the time the sensor is allowed to see the image, making your shot quite dark. To compensate, you'd need to open your aperture by three stops to return to a brightness similar to what you had before the change. Each shutter change approximately doubles the amount of light allowed in, the same way your f-stop does. So the shutter speed might be:

1/30, 1/50, 1/125, 1/250, 1/500.

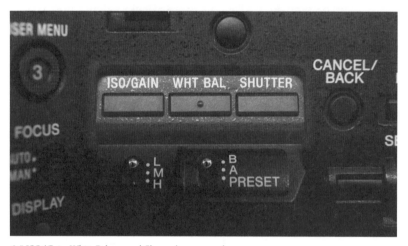

3.5 ISO/Gain, White Balance, and Shutter buttons on the camera

Determine the shutter speed you should be recording on by doubling your frame rate. Shooting at 25 fps means 1/50th of a second for your shutter.

FOCUS

Focus on the camera can be set to either automatic or manual. You're a professional, though; you want the best-looking shots you can achieve, and you want to be in control of what is in focus in your image at any given time. So keep it on manual.

There are two types of zoom lenses: parfocal and varifocal. To focus on a parfocal zoom lens, simply zoom in on your object (or your talent's eyes), move the focal ring until it's sharp on the monitor or viewfinder, and zoom back out to the desired shot size. Varifocal lenses, however, like most DSLR lenses, change their focus point as the focal length changes, so zooming into focus isn't an option. Some new cameras have a magnifying button that will punch in or magnify the image and then allow you to check or alter focus. With cameras fitted with prime lenses, the focus can either be achieved by measuring the distance from the focal plane of the camera's sensor to the person or object, or by using the magnifying function as mentioned above.

"Pulling focus" or "rack focus" refers to changing the focus from one object or person to another, or following just one person as they move toward or away from camera. It involves setting the focus for person A and then for person B. On a given cue, the focus wheel can be turned to its new mark, and the focus shifts to the new object. Or, as mentioned, it could be just a single person walking toward camera, and the focus has to be pulled in order to keep them sharp throughout the length of the shot. The camera operator can pull the focus; on larger shoots this job falls to the focus puller or 1st assistant camera (1st AC). Pulling focus can be an easy job or a hard one depending on what f-stop you are working on. Imagine filming someone moving at night and using a fairly wide aperture, say, f/2.8. The depth of field (the area of what's in focus) around them is going to be fairly small. A tough job for the

3.6 Follow focus wheel in action

3.7 A remote follow focus unit

camera assistant or camera operator! The move can be rehearsed, and marks can be put down on the floor to help with that. A follow focus wheel is used to mark the focus points so the assistant can see what to pull from and to.

Pulling focus can also be achieved remotely by using a wireless follow focus unit. This is especially useful if the camera is on a Steadicam or crane, or if space around the camera is tight and the focus puller can't position themselves near the camera.

PRIME LENSES / ZOOM LENSES

Prime lenses are lenses that are of a fixed focal length. It is not possible to zoom in or zoom out with a prime lens. If you want a wider or closer shot, pick up your camera and physically move forward or backward or change to a different focal-length lens. Prime lenses come in a wide variety of focal sizes. A standard set — 18mm, 25mm, 32mm, 40mm, 50mm, 85mm, 100mm, 135mm —will cover you for most setups. Being primes, they have less glass in the body of the lens for the light to pass through, so the quality of the image is better. They are, however, a lot more expensive to rent.

Primes are great for shooting drama, but shouldn't be considered for documentaries or anything that is shooting "on the fly." You would need the flexibility of a zoom to be able to zoom in quickly and capture new shots as they happen.

3.8 A set of prime lenses

3.9 A zoom lens

3.10

3.11

3.12

3.13

3.14

3.15

3.16

3.17

WIDE AND LONG LENSES

You could choose to shoot your wide shots on the 18mm or the 25mm. For actor close-ups, you might look to the 40mm or 50mm. Then for insert shots or long-lens, point-of-view shots, you might use the 100mm, or 135mm. This is just a loose guide, of course. Some directors like to shoot their wides on a 50mm and their actors with 85mm. A long lens — anything about 85mm and up — flattens out the image and makes objects that are far apart seem closer together.

Some action scenes are shot with long lenses to make it look like the actor is very close to danger, like a huge explosion going off behind them, or a crashing car rolling down a pedestrian-heavy street. Shooting on a 135mm lens would make the action look like it was only feet away, enhancing the tension. Long lenses are also good to show a certain amount of energy. Filming your actor running on a long lens with lots of foreground objects whizzing through the frame conveys a much greater sense of speed. This is a good example of using your tools to help tell your story.

3.18 A long lens compressing the action to make things look closer than they appear

Wide-angle lenses — 18mm, 25mm — can also distort an image if used in certain conditions. When put too close to the actor's face, a wide angle could enhance features that are unflattering and should not be emphasized. You might look at filming the shot on a 50mm lens or higher. If you're shooting a horror movie or intense drama where you want the villain to look scary, imposing, or threatening, you might shoot your serial killer or zombie with an 18mm lens six inches from their face! This way, you're making your camera and lens choices work for you. Wider lenses are also great for capturing wide master shots or vistas and ensuring every element is in frame.

3.19 18mm. The wide angle lens enhances features that could be unflattering.

3.20 50mm. The longer lens offers a more flattering image of our actor.

FILTERS

Filters can come in two forms. One internally within the camera body or externally as a piece of glass that can be placed in front of the camera by sliding into the attached matte box.

NEUTRAL DENSITY FILTERS:

Some cameras come fitted with a selection of built-in neutral density (ND) filters of varying strengths. Neutral-density filters reduce the intensity of the light, yielding no changes in color rendition. The director of photography can use them to reduce light in order to change aperture or shutter settings. ND filters are like a pair of sunglasses. When things become too bright outside, you put sunglasses on to see better and to not have to squint. They come in various strengths and different densities to help cut out the light entering the camera. Common strengths are 0.3 ND, the equivalent of 1 full stop down in aperture; 0.6 ND, 2 full stops; and 0.9, 3 full stops. ND filters are basically gray glass. When a filter is placed in front of the camera, the camera assistant will mark up the side of the matte box with tape or a sticker displaying what filter is being used. This lets everyone in the camera department know what filters are in play without having to remove them each time to check.

3.21 Filter labels in action

ND filters enable you to have more control of the f-stop; use them to reduce your depth of field. Say you have some foreground action that isn't as soft or out of focus as you would like, or the background is still quite visible. You have your image at a given exposure, say, f/8, which you would like to be at f/4. Using the camera's ND filters or a glass version in the matte box at a strength of 0.6 darkens your image. Then, you can open the aperture to f/4 (2 full stops wider than f/8, equivalent to 0.6) to achieve the same image brightness you had before applying the ND filters. Now your aperture is wider and your depth of field therefore smaller. So you are using the ND filters to give you that shallow depth of field look and move away from the TV news feel of deep focus.

Full ND filters are gray all over the glass from top to bottom. There are also filters which are graduated; they are gray at the top and gradually fade to clear at the bottom. These filters are great for filming skies where the foreground image of the subject is well exposed, but the sky is blowing out or overexposed and reading as white. Let's say the foreground action is exposing nicely for f/5.6, and the sky is three stops over and needs to be exposed at f/16 to see the detail and clouds properly. If you stop down your aperture to f/16 for the sky, your foreground will be too dark. So what could possibly be the solution? Graduated ND filters! Find a filter with a strength of 0.9, place it in front of the camera, and then the sky and the foreground will be properly exposed. Graduated filters come in two forms with differing graduation. One is soft edge (S/E), with a smooth, soft fading out of the ND or filter color; the other is hard edge (H/E), which is a more straight, hard line between the filter and the clear side.

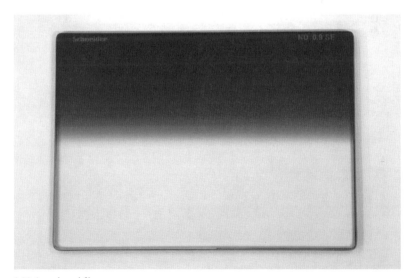

3.22 A graduated filter

Another good use of ND filters is for dramatic effect. Maybe your sky and foreground are correctly exposed already, but you choose to put a 0.9 ND grad filter in front of the camera. Now, if you're filming on an overcast day with white clouds, putting on a 0.9 ND graduated filter will send your white clouds to gray, or gray clouds to very dark gray, giving the impression of an approaching storm. I've even used them heavily on a nice, clear, blue sky. Adding graduated ND filters to the camera made the sky a darker blue at the top of frame, slowly fading to a lighter blue at the bottom. They have many uses to the DP, and it is about just being creative with the tools available.

3.23 Image with no graduated filter

3.24 Image with graduated filter

POLARIZER FILTERS:

When light is reflected it bounces around or vibrates everywhere. A polarizer filter passes only the light coming in from one direction. This is very useful when you are filming glass or anything with a reflection. A polarizer can be rotated in the matte box in various degrees to help reduce reflections on glass or reflected objects. It also helps darken the image by about 1½ to 2 stops and boost colors when filming skies and water. It does this by filtering out the polarized component of the light and increasing the contrast in the image.

3.25 Image with no polarizer filter

3.26 Image with polarizer filter

DIFFUSION FILTERS:

Black Pro-Mists are a favorite of mine and are an example of a diffusion filter. They come in various strengths and types, including 1/8, 1/4, 1/2, and full. They are a soft-focus filter, reducing the value in the highlights and lowering the contrast. It does mean a little loss in detail, but some camera operators constantly use a 1/8 strength filter in front of the camera just to take that edge off the super sharp and clear high-resolution images. Diffusion filters also help reduce wrinkles and blemishes in the face of your talent. They also give a soft, tiny halo effect to highlights, which can add a magical or enlightened look to the shot.

3.27 Image with no diffusion filter

3.28 Image with diffusion filter

3.29 Image with no diffusion filter

3.30 Image with diffusion filter

CINEMATOGRAPHY

Before we start talking about lighting, gear, and what different images might mean, perhaps we should first ask: What is cinematography?

Cinematography is the art of balancing light, camera, colors, and performers, all mixed together in every single frame. The cinematographer or director of photography (DP) works very closely with the director to establish the mood and tone of the film through camera placement / movement, composition, color usage, darkness and light, and overall feel. The lights you choose create a mood for the piece and get good exposure too.

I see each shot as a little puzzle to solve; it's a jigsaw or a crossword, and with each new shot the puzzle resets itself. Each shot and its solution are completely different from the next, which bring their own challenges. Some filmmakers know technical details such as lenses, crop factors, resolution, etc., but have little understanding of feeling or the abstract. Others are all feeling and emotion without much understanding of technical aspects and matters of execution. Of course, a good balance is somewhere in between.

With today's cameras, it is possible to get a "passively good-looking image." Out of the box, the new DSLRs can give great-looking images. Blacks are crushed a little; there's a shallow depth of field; etc. But the more important factor is: Can you tell a story? Can you shoot something that holds together and is compelling? There is more to cinematography than beautiful-looking images. This is worth remembering. It is best to understand the fundamentals beforehand, then when on set the feeling and the emotion of the scene can guide you in the right direction.

There are a number of factors to consider under the subject of cinematography, and all will come into play to help you compose your image. It starts with the script initially and how you analyze and break the text down. How does it make you feel? What are your thoughts on the story, emotion, tone? These will all inform your ideas on camera placement and style. What available gear might help capture this vision, all while incorporating the practical needs of the set? You're not necessarily going for nice images, but the right images for the film's subject and style. In other words, they have to be the appropriate pictures for the film. If they happen to look good in the process, all the better.

If you are interested in cinematography, being a student doesn't start with being on set. It starts by looking around you in your everyday conditions. How does light fall in certain places? What does it look like in your front room at a given time of day? What color is the light? How hard or soft is it?

LIGHTING PLANS AND GEAR LISTS

Once you've visited your location and talked to the director about how they envisage the film, put together a lighting diagram of how you plan to execute the scenes. Lighting schematics are an excellent step in your preparation, as they take all the hard work and thinking required away from the set, where time costs money. Here's an example of a lighting schematic. It was an office set with two people talking over a desk that was positioned by a window. The second picture (next page) is a still from the film itself to see how all the lights matched up.

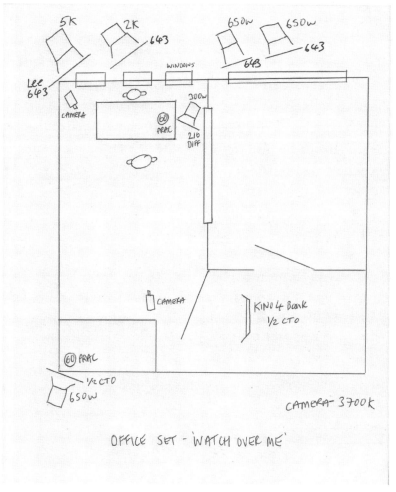

3.31 Lighting plan

3.32 Still taken from action film *Watch Over Me*

Lighting schematics always show the overhead view of the set layout so any points of note can be seen clearly. From this lighting plan, you can compile a list of all the gear you think you'll need for the shoot. In most cases, the first pass of a gear list is a "wish list" until the producer sees it and tells you the budget won't allow for such things. So then you're forced to be a little more creative and see what can be done for less money.

GEAR

What's great about cinematography is that you don't need big, expensive gear to do amazing work. Sometimes you might require large 18K HMI lights and generators, and sometimes all a shot will need is considered composition and natural light. Let's have a brief look at some types of lights you might find yourself using as tools of the cinematographer's trade.

There are four types of artificial sources that you can use for your lighting setups:

- Tungsten
- HMI
- Fluorescent
- LED

TUNGSTEN:

Tungsten units are normally cheaper to rent, and are balanced to a color temperature of 3200K. They take their name from the tungsten filament inside the lamp that glows when heated. Tungsten lights can get very hot and can burn through gels placed in front if attached too close. Here's an example of a tungsten lamp, a 2K Blonde.

3.33 A 2K blonde

HMI:

HMIs (Hydrargyrum Medium-Arc Iodides) use what is called an arc lamp rather than an incandescent bulb, like tungsten lamps. They can be expensive to rent; they're cooler than tungsten lights and don't require any gels to be attached to convert to daylight-balanced scenes. They do come with a ballast to make them run, which fires up the light and regulates the arc inside.

3.34 An HMI daylight balanced light

Daylight-balanced lamps have a color temperature of 5600K.

FLUORESCENT:

Fluorescent lamps work by ionizing mercury vapor in a glass tube. These tubes come in various color temperatures that make them a great tool for cinematographers. Various companies now manufacture this commercial soft-light source consisting of two or four long fluorescent tubes in one unit.

3.35 A kino flo soft light

LED LIGHT PANELS:

LED stands for Light-Emitting Diode. They are small units, some about one square foot, and can be battery- or grid-powered with adjustable dials for color temperature and intensity. They are very lightweight and versatile units, and can therefore be very expensive to rent or buy. Cheaper versions have a tendency to give off a green tint, so beware.

3.36 An LED light

TYPES OF LIGHT – HARD AND SOFT

Depending on the source of the light you have to play with, whether it is natural like the sun or artificial like electrical lamps, it will either be a "hard" or a "soft" light.

The best way to see the difference between hard and soft light is to watch the shadows on the floor outside when the sun is shining. All objects will cast a shadow. If the source is direct with no clouds in between, the shadows cast will all have a hard edge and a well-defined shadow on the floor. When the sun goes behind the clouds, the light becomes DIFFUSED and turns into soft light. The shadows cast from those objects will now have a softer, less-defined edge to them. That's hard and soft light.

Hard light comes from a small light source falling directly onto a subject. When someone stands in hard light, the shadows on their face are harsh and dark. This produces a high contrast that emphasizes wrinkles, skin issues, and bags under their eyes.

Soft light is less direct, and shadows are smoother, making the person's face look better. Soft light comes from a larger source usually reflected or diffused in some way.

There are three ways to get soft light, and each can be used depending on budgetary and space considerations.

1. Rent a light that produces commercially soft light direct from the unit. Kino Flo is the most common brand, consisting of 2/4 fluorescent tubes in a plastic casing. They can come in either color temperature you choose. A Diva is a type of soft light source that is also dimmable for you to control the intensity. A Celeb light is programmable with intensities and changeable color also.

3.37 A kino flo soft light

2. You can BOUNCE the hard source light off a white poly-board or a white wall directed at your action. The larger the board, the softer the light.

3.38 Bounce light in action

3. You can direct the hard light through a DIFFUSION filter or frame. This is a slightly more direct route, enabling you to control the light better than bouncing, which can scatter the light all over the room.

3.39 A diffusion frame softening light

Diffusion frames are worth looking at if shooting outside. Large six-square-foot, eight-square-foot, and twelve-square-foot frames hold diffusion material such as silk or a thin, white cloth to turn the harsh sunlight into a more flattering soft light when placed overhead. You still keep the direction of the light, but it's softer and wraps around the face in a more pleasing way for your actors. Check out the pictures below to see the diffusion frame on set, and then the before-and-after to see how diffusion softens the light on the actor's face.

3.40 A 6x6 diffusion frame above our actor softening the hard sunlight

3.41 A shot of our actor without the diffusion frame

3.42 The same shot but with the diffusion frame softening shadows

Hard light is easier to control with flags to remove light from nearby walls or wherever you don't want it falling. Soft light is a little harder to flag and control since it's being scattered over a wider area. There are pros and cons to using hard and soft light; it all comes down to the source of the light that is in the scene, and what look and feel you are going for within your environment.

COLOR TEMPERATURE

I'm going to try and make this as simple as I can, as this is a big, tough subject! But knowing the basics of color temperature can definitely help you make better pictures. If you're new to this, it does take a while to understand this topic. But you have to read, then try things out, read again, try again, and eventually you'll get it. Trust me . . .

Imagine we have a black, solid metal object. When this solid is slowly heated, it will glow a certain color when it gets to a particular temperature. These temperatures are measured in degrees Kelvin (K). So we have a scale of various environments and sources that all give off different temperatures and therefore colors of light. For example, sunrises are orange, and night time has a blueish tint.

Our eyes can make adjustments for these differences, but the camera needs to be told what it's looking at. If it's wrong, it will produce a color cast over your image, which I'm sure we've all seen before when things might look a little blue or orange. The thing to first understand is the color and the temperature work in opposition to one another. Although we normally think of hot being red and cool being blue, on a color temperature scale, something getting hotter glows blue and something cooling down turns to more of a red. Take a look at the color temperature scale on the inside back cover of this book (fig. 3.43).

As you can see, we have candlelight at 1800K, sunrise / sunset at 2000K, early morning at 4000K, average daylight sun at 5600K, and average shade at 9000K.

If the source of the light you are using is higher on the scale than what the camera is set to, you'll get a blue color cast on your image or from that source. If the source is lower than the camera setting, you'll get an orange color cast. We'll figure out how we can use this scale when shooting in a moment.

Cameras normally have various settings for color temperature — also known as the "white balance." It's called "white balance" because you are telling the camera what white is. Our eyes adjust or balance naturally and see white as white in any situation, but the camera needs to be told what it is filming. So the four settings you might find on your camera are:

Daylight preset — measured at 5600K

Tungsten preset — measured at 3200K

Fluorescent preset — measured at 4300K

Manually set through balancing to white card or dial

As daylight and tungsten are the main two situations that you'll find yourself shooting in, you can select each one via the presets. The manual function allows you to tell the camera the exact color of white it is seeing by placing a white card in front of the camera and holding down the white balance (WB) button for roughly 3 seconds, until it flashes "set." Some DSLR cameras have more settings than this, allowing for cloudy (7000K) and overcast (9000K) conditions, among others. Some cameras allow you to manually dial in the color temperature you'd like. Maybe the presets are a little warm or cool for your liking, so you change the color temperature to a different setting.

Daylight refers to filming conditions outside, but what does *tungsten* mean? Tungsten takes its name from the tungsten filament found inside a normal household lightbulb. It is this filament that when heated gives off the orange glow. If you are filming inside with lights on, set your camera to tungsten. If you are filming outside, then set your camera to daylight. Now, the problems arise when you are mixing these sources in the SAME scene. What do you set it to?

Consider this chart a simple guide to what color casts happen and when.

Camera setting	Source light	Color cast
Daylight	Daylight	None
Daylight	Tungsten	Orange
Tungsten	Tungsten	None
Tungsten	Daylight	Blue

You might have already seen this happen in the projects you may be shooting. You're filming inside on a tungsten setting and a window gets in your frame, allowing daylight to creep into your shot. This daylight now looks all blue. Or vice-versa: You may be filming outside and someone in a nearby house has a light on; this light will then look a little orange. Mixing these color temperatures can be troublesome if it's not the look you're aiming for. This is where color-correction lighting gels come in. If you turn to the inside cover at the front of the book (fig. 3.44), you'll see an example of a shot taken in daylight conditions, but with the color temperature set to tungsten. See the blue cast?

GELS

Gels come in various types of colors and strengths. There are simply too many to list, so we will focus on the main set you might find yourself requiring. Gels can be used for correcting the temperature of the lights you're using, or simply for creating mood. Maybe you don't have a color cast problem as all the lights you are using are tungsten, but you want the one at the back to be red and the light above to be a little green . . . Who knows? This is what is so great about cinematography: it is all up to the choice of the artist.

3.45 A light with a gel applied

Some common lighting gels are:

Full CTB (Color Temperature Blue) — Used to convert tungsten sources to daylight or to turn HMI sources blue, to create moonlight, for example.
    1/2 CTB
    1/4 CTB
    1/8 CTB

Full CTO (Color Temperature Orange) — Used to convert daylight HMI's to tungsten, or to lower the temperature of tungsten sources to sunrise / sunset, for example.

> 1/2 CTO
> 1/4 CTO
> 1/8 CTO

Neutral Density (ND) — Reduces the intensity of light without changing the color. They are very similar to the ND filters mentioned before, but this time in dark gray gel form for lights. These gels are used to adjust the output from just one light in a scene, whereas adding ND in the camera will adjust the output of all lights by darkening the image overall. ND gels also come in various strengths to reduce intensity. The 1-stop change listed below is equivalent to what you would have to do to your camera's aperture to get the same effect.

> ND 0.3 (1-stop change)
> ND 0.6 (2-stop change)
> ND 0.9 (3-stop change)

Diffusion — Diffusion is a white or frosted gel, a little like tracing paper. It is used to soften or "diffuse" the light from a hard source. This gel can be clipped to the front of a light or be made into a larger frame to be positioned in front of the hard source light to make it soft. There are many types of diffusion, and varying strengths.

PUTTING IT INTO PRACTICE

Let's assume you are filming inside and there is daylight coming in the windows for a good portion of the shot. The scene has no practical light from bulbs or lamps, so it is a little dark. To bring up the exposure, we bring out one of our lights, maybe a 2K blonde. This light is tungsten-balanced; left uncorrected, it will read orange in the image when our camera is set to daylight (which it should be, as most of our light in the scene is daylight sourced). To move the color temperature of the blonde light up toward daylight, from 3200K to 5600K, we could add a full CTB gel. A full color temperature blue gel would convert the tungsten light to daylight so its output would match the light from the window. Now we can light our scene, whatever that might be, and everything will be even from a color temperature point of view. But sometimes daylight isn't 5600K. Throughout the day it does go up and down, as we can see from early morning and evening times on the chart. So if the daylight at the time is more like 4600K, we could try putting a 1/2 CTB on the blonde, which would only half convert the blonde to daylight. This is all up to your judgment.

The alternative would be to rent an HMI (Hydrargyrum Medium-Arc Iodide) daylight-balanced light, and then you won't need to correct it at all.

Let's look at another example. Say you're shooting a candle. I personally want that candlelight to read a little orange. Candlelight is 1800K on your color temperature scale, lower than a 3200K tungsten setting. Remembering that every source that is lower than the camera setting is going to read a little orange, I know if I set my camera to tungsten, that candle will read a little orange since tungsten is a little higher on the scale than candlelight. However, if I did a white balance card reading in that environment, the camera would see the present orange cast and electronically add blue to the mix to balance the orange tint and make the scene whiter. The camera thinks it's helping you by eliminating the color cast the source is giving you. I don't want my candle to be white; I want it orange. Remember, if the source light matches the color-temperature setting on the camera, any white light will read as white. In our candle situation, when white balancing, the camera would be set to about 1800K, casting out our orange light for good! So what would happen to our candlelight if the camera was not set to tungsten, but to daylight? Remembering every source lower than the camera setting gives off an orange tint, the candle will now read as . . . VERY orange. This is something you might want to try. If you were shooting on a camera with color-temperature adjustment, you might find 3200K at tungsten not orange enough, but a 5600K daylight setting too much. So you could dial it down to 4000K. Then you might have an orange tint you are pleased with.

3.46 Our ideal Christmas scene

Have a look at this illustration of a house at Christmas. Say we want a Christmassy feel to this shot, and that the director has asked for the exterior to be a little blue, as if the moon is casting a blue tint over everything, while the interior needs to have an orangey glow from the fireplace. You could pretend we're making a Christmas ad for TV. How can we use our lights, gels, and camera settings to achieve this?

We have a blonde (tungsten) light inside the room to lift exposure and to simulate our light from the fireplace. The fire itself wouldn't give us anything bright enough to really use, so we'd enhance it artificially. Now, do we need to gel this light? To give the feel of firelight and make it look warm and cozy, the camera's white balance must be set properly.

We have also placed an HMI outside to light the side of the house and give our moonlight effect. Do we need to gel this light too? Let's have a look at the two scenarios.

CAMERA SETTING 1: TUNGSTEN

With this setting, the blonde lamp inside will need gelling with CTO since the camera and source light will match. Will the HMI outside need gelling too? Well, maybe not, since the HMI will automatically give a bluish color cast with the camera set to tungsten. If, however, for artistic reasons you wanted it to look even bluer (sometimes referred to as "American night" since Hollywood movies always seem to have blue moonlight), you could add a little CTB to help, maybe a ¼ CTB.

CAMERA SETTING 2: DAYLIGHT

If we set it to daylight, the blonde lamp inside will give off an orange cast naturally, so you might not need to gel it if it's giving you the look you are after. The HMI outside, though, will now be reading as white light (since camera setting and source match) and will not produce the blue-moonlight feel the director is after. You might need to gel the HMI a ¼ or ½ CTB to give it that moonlight feel.

SHOT SIZES

There are standard industry shot sizes that we can choose to help tell our story. This film grammar was established in Hollywood in the 1920s, in the early days of film. We have the main three:
- Wide / master
- Medium
- Close-up

WIDE / MASTER:

The wide helps establish where we are: what is around us, where the characters are in relation to each other, and a sense of scale and place. The wide needn't be the first shot in the edited sequence, but it should ideally come fairly near the front to set things up. Never underestimate the power of a wide / master shot. Sometimes directors fall into the trap of not showing it well, assuming the audience knows the surroundings. The orientation of the scene might be confusing, but the director is unable to think beyond his or her memory of where everything was on filming day.

3.47 Wide shot

MEDIUM:

The medium allows us to get a little closer to our characters and objects. We see them in more detail, particularly their eyes, allowing us to identify with them while keeping a sense of place. Hand and arm gestures play well in a medium shot but might not do so in a wide without seeing the character's eyes simultaneously. And they would be out of frame and lost in a close-up. The medium gives us a good sense of the background and shows us the character's body language too.

3.48 Medium shot

CLOSE-UP:

Close-ups convey the emotional beats of a scene. Small nuances of performance can be seen wonderfully in a close-up. That tiny bite of a lip, the squint of an eye . . . a close-up should ideally be saved for the most emotional parts of a scene.

3.49 Close-up

Sprinkled around those initial three shot sizes we also have:

EXTREME WIDE:

The extreme wide conveys distance. Think of epic films like *Lawrence of Arabia* (1962). If someone was alone in a desert, a standard wide shot wouldn't convey the size of the landscape or the distance around our character. But an extreme wide would tell us how far they have to walk or who or what is around them.

3.50 Extreme wide shot

COWBOY (MEDIUM UP FROM THE MID-THIGH):

The cowboy's name is derived from the Western genre. When filming a cowboy in the frame, a medium shot would cut off at the waist and not allow the camera to see the gun holster that our hero might be reaching for. Alternatively, a wide would be too far back and we might see the guns, but they might not be too clear in the frame.

3.51 Cowboy shot

TWO SHOT:

The two shot features more than one actor and allows the audience to do the editing by choosing who to focus on. This shot lets the audience see reactions of the other characters immediately. A two shot also binds two characters together nicely, suggesting that there is a connection between them.

3.52 Two shot

MEDIUM CLOSE-UP:

The medium close-up is fairly self-explanatory. It's halfway between a medium and a close-up. Normally cutting the actor off mid-chest, it's getting physically closer for those emotional beats.

3.53 Medium close-up

EXTREME CLOSE-UP:

The extreme close-up would crop the actor's face above the eye and below the mouth. This is very close and not particularly flattering. A good guideline is the "arm's-length rule." If you were to face someone and hold your outstretched arm on their shoulder, this would keep you at a comfortable distance from them. To the eye, the other person would appear to you like a close-up shot would to the camera. Now, there are only a few reasons why you would venture in closer

3.54 Extreme close-up

than this in everyday life. One is to get intimate with someone in an emotional encounter, or to confront them in a threatening manner. So you should have a good reason to go in this close.

POINT OF VIEW:

A point-of-view shot or POV is when we see what the character sees. This can be any of the shot sizes listed above. Compositionally, you could place your object or subject more in the center of the frame, rather than use the conventional Rule of Thirds (more on that shortly). This way the audience has no doubt it's seeing what the character is seeing.

OVER-THE-SHOULDER (OTS):

Over-the-shoulder is the name given to shots where the camera is literally placed over the character's shoulder so we see what they see. When you have characters talking to each other or looking at things, you can decide whether you shoot the angle "clean," without the shoulder in frame, or as an OTS including a shoulder. OTS shots can add a few nice touches to your story. They give a sense of someone listening; we can literally see their ear, and it aids orientation by revealing how far away the other person is from our character.

3.55 A well-composed over-the-shoulder shot

Each of these shot sizes are used to help propel the story forward. They help the audience to relate and become attached to or detached from the characters.

It's up to the director and cameraman to decide what shots to use and why. Consider the Clint Eastwood film *The Bridges of Madison County* (1995). Eastwood plays a *National Geographic* photographer visiting Iowa to photograph all the covered bridges in the local area. When lost on his travels, he calls on housewife Meryl Streep to ask for directions. As the two strangers talk, she stands on her front porch and Clint by his truck. The scene is shot in the beginning by using mostly wide shots positioned over-the-shoulder. There is a distance here: she doesn't know him and he doesn't know her. As the scene progresses, we slowly start to cut in tighter, moving to cowboy-size shots and then finally to medium close-ups. Eastwood lets the emotion and story direct his shots. We see what the characters see, then we feel what the characters feel.

3.56 Wide over-the-shoulder shot from Eastwood's point of view

3.57 Wide over-the-shoulder shot from Streep's point of view

3.58 Slowly moving in closer

3.59 Closer in on Eastwood with a cowboy shot

3.60 Closer still, with a medium close-up on Streep

3.61 Eastwood's matching medium close-up shot

COMPOSITION

Composition is the frame. Everything that you see or don't see within your shot. Composition is a very important part of cinematography; use it to tell your story. A good example of storytelling through simple composition can be found below:

3.62 A swimmer framed on the bottom third

3.63 A swimmer framed on the top third, creating a sense of tension

The first picture presents a person swimming in the sea. It's a beautiful day and everything seems fine.

But what about the second picture? What are you thinking when you look at this frame? Is the swimmer somehow in danger now? It's not like we know any more information. But somehow, through the simple power of composition, we tell a different story. Maybe the swimmer is out of their depth? For me, I see a shark attack coming. The water feels deeper, and monsters or unseen things live in the deep . . . All that has happened technically is the camera has tilted down to place the swimmer in the top of the frame, but it brings a whole new set of meanings with it.

The Rule of Thirds is a compositional tool camera operators use to align their images. Early painters and still photographers used it before filmmakers adopted it. The best way to think of it is as a tic-tac-toe board. Imagine placing four lines over your image to produce nine squares. Then it's about simply placing objects, people, or locations on those lines. Placing these things on the lines looks good, but having objects or people positioned where the lines cross is even better. Check out this still (next page) from *Jurassic Park* (1993) to see it in action. The car and the *T. rex*'s feet are all positioned in the bottom third. The *T. rex*'s mouth is where the left third and the top third cross, and Sam Neill's Alan Grant character is positioned in the right third.

3.64 A frame from *Jurassic Park* with the Rule of Thirds in action

Look at the picture below:

3.65 Vacation photo badly framed

This is what most people's vacation photos look like. The horizon is cutting the picture in half, with the person standing dead center. Now have a look at this:

3.66 That's better . . . a vacation photo using rule of thirds

Using the Rule of Thirds and adjusting the frame can make the same image look a lot better. The horizon is now in the bottom third. The boat is also in the bottom third, but placed where the left third meets the bottom third. The person is placed in the right third with their head and (most importantly) their eyes where the right third meets the top third. Great composition! You see this everywhere: on TV shows and in movies, and even in paintings and photographs.

This framing tool makes the audience feel comfortable. There is enough space around the character to breathe and move, and the audience knows where everything is. The trick is to know when to break these rules. We looked at over-the-shoulder shots earlier; look at the shot below and see if you can say how the composition could be improved.

3.67 A poorly composed over-the-shoulder frame. How could you make this better?

ASPECT RATIO

Aspect ratio refers to the height and width of the frame that you choose to shoot your film in. It is normally presented numerically as two different numbers with a colon in between. The main ratios to be aware of are 1.33:1 or 4:3, 16:9, 1.85:1, and 2.35:1.

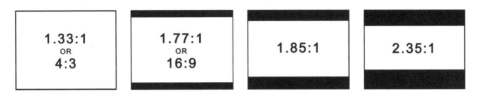

3.68 The four main aspect ratios

The first value represents the width, and the second number, after the colon, gives us the height. Back in the early days of silent filmmaking, all films were 4:3, or more accurately, 1.33:1. The advent of sound meant they had to alter the size of the screen to fit the soundtrack on the side of the film reel. The figure became 1.37:1, and was dubbed "Academy ratio" in 1932.

Things stayed like this for 20 years or more until the introduction of television in the 1950s. Theatre bosses got a little nervous and tried to entice audiences back to the cinemas and away from their TV sets. What they offered was the "widescreen" that we know and use to this day.

Whether a film decides to shoot 4:3, or widescreen using the ratios of 1.85:1 or 2.35:1 (using anamorphic lenses or not) is a decision the director / DP and producers make based on the script, aesthetics, and budget. For more TV and video–based work, the standard aspect ratio is 16:9. 16:9 is now the universal format for video, and has a filmic aspect ratio equivalent of 1.77:1. Some film-makers opt to shoot and frame for a 2.35:1 aspect ratio when shooting within the 16:9 frame and use markers in the viewfinder and monitor to set the correct shot. The unused part of the frame is blacked out during post-production.

For the majority of work, 16:9 works wonderfully as an aspect ratio. Traditionally, if the subject matter is drama-based or more of a human-interest story, a 16:9 or 1.85:1 aspect ratio is used. Or a project whose action or subject matter necessitates a wider frame might arise. Maybe the film is set against some epic landscapes providing wonderful vistas or features long spaceships doing battle, so a choice of 2.35:1 or an even wider 2.39:1 could be used. I have filmed a couple of dramas and an action film where the decision was made to use the wider 2.35:1 frame to capture the film. It all comes down to aesthetics, the subject matter, and what works for the director and DP. We discuss using the 2.35:1 ratio again in the chapter "Common Traits of Student Films"; if you do decide to use a wider frame, make sure it is planned and shot accordingly, rather than cropping the image in post and losing half your frame.

Here are a few examples of aspect ratio in play. *It's a Wonderful Life* (1946) was framed in 4:3 before the introduction of widescreen; *Atonement* (2007) utilizes the 1.85:1 ratio to tell a more intimate love story; and finally, *Dances With Wolves* (1990) uses all of the frame to capture those gorgeous vistas in 2.35:1.

3.69 *It's a Wonderful Life*

3.70 *Atonement*

3.71 *Dances With Wolves*

HOW TO LIGHT – 3-POINT LIGHTING

Most lighting is either supporting or adding to what's already there on location. You then take your cues on the intensity of the light, and the color from that. Or maybe you're starting from scratch on a set or studio.

Start with motivated light or a "supposed" motivated light source already established in the environment. It could be a window or a practical light (a light the characters can see), or something the audience could justify as a source of light. Is it hard light or soft? What color is it?

You'll find that 95% of the time, you light with motivational sources — a window, a doorway, a table lamp. Use these as your motivation to light your scene. Maybe that table light alone isn't enough to key your actor, but a 300W tungsten light from a similar angle and color will be. The audience knows the table light is there, and when they see the light on the actor's face in the next shot they know it must be coming from the table light. There: easy, motivated light sources!

However, and there is always a however, sometimes having a light somewhere in a scene or on an actor might *feel* right, but there's no obvious source, so technically it shouldn't be there. So should we have it? The answer is yes. This is one of those instances when you have to go with your gut. You might be shooting a horror movie; you can create wonderful shafts of light for your character to walk through. Lots of darkness and shadow . . . But what's causing those shafts? Where is that light coming from? The answer is the same place the spooky music is. It's very easy for students to learn that something has to be a particular way, or it's wrong. They can get hung up on that and miss wonderful chances to create and shoot some bold images. Most of what you do should indeed come from a moti- vated place, but there is always room for artistic interpretation. Rules are good, but know when to have the confidence to break them! A good line to remember is: 95% motivation, but emotion trumps realism.

Three-point lighting goes back to the old studio system in the 1930s where actors were all lit a certain way. I like to think of it as a foundation, a starting point that you can move on from and tweak. The three main lights in three-point lighting are:

KEY LIGHT:

The main light source in the scene. This can be the light from the window, the desk lamp, or if you're outside, the sun. It can be artificial light or natural light. A good starting position for the key light is at a 45-degree angle between your talent and the camera, and at a 45-degree downward angle. This is commonly known as the 45/45 rule. ("Rule" of course meaning a good starting point.) You set the exposure on the camera by this key light.

3.72

BACKLIGHT:

Backlight, as its name suggests, backlights the actors. Placed behind them, the light creates a rim or halo light around their back, head, or shoulders to bring them out from the background. Picture a person wearing a black suit in a dark room. A backlight would define them and show us their form against the darkness.

3.73

FILL LIGHT:

Fill light "fills" in the shadows caused by the key light. It's normally placed on the opposite side of the camera to the key light, and is of a lesser intensity than the key light in order for us to see the effects of the key light. If the fill light was the same intensity, you wouldn't see any shadows at all since the two lights would balance each other out. The fill light helps set the mood.

3.74

Below is a diagram showing the placement of the three lights on an actor. You can see the key light is placed at a 45-degree angle to the actor.

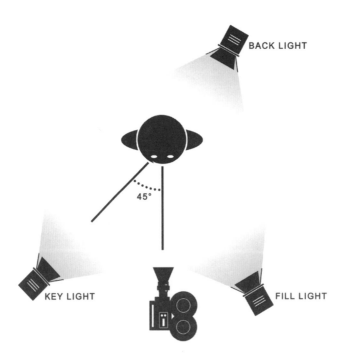

3.75

Here's an overhead view of our kitchen scene to see it all in practice.

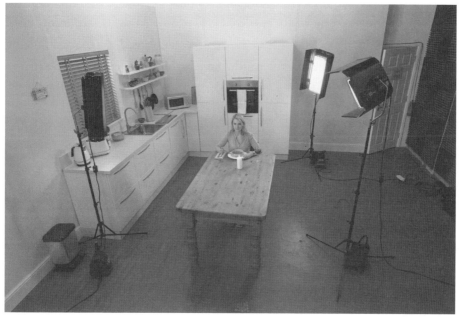

3.76

You don't need all three; it completely depends on what you're shooting. Maybe you just want to lift the exposure level. You might bounce some lights onto the ceiling or into some poly-boards to fill the shot, and that's the only lighting you do. What would you end up with if you only backlit your subject with no other lights in the room? A silhouette. That backlight would become your key light since it would then be the main light source in the scene.

SHOOTING ON THE FILL SIDE

A few simple guidelines — not rules, guidelines — to keep in mind. When setting up a shot, try to keep your camera shooting the actor on their fill side, the darker side of the face. This way the key light coming in from the opposite side of their face will wrap around the face, gradually getting a little darker as it moves toward the camera and falls off. This helps show the key light better and reveals texture on the actor or object. It makes things look a little more dynamic.

Look at this screenshot from the Robert Downey, Jr. movie *The Judge* (2014). This close-up of Downey shows it all in play: the motivated light source, shooting on the fill side, his eyes on the top third, and a highlight in his eyes to make him look even better!

3.77 Still from *The Judge* showing the highlight in the eyes and motivated source light

CONTROLLING LIGHT

Controlling your light source is where your skills really come into play. Illuminating your actor or subject in the frame is one thing, but taking light away is another. When I first started out, I would place my lights, and if they spilled all over the wall behind the actor or made something look too bright or unflattering, I assumed that I must have positioned the light in the wrong place. What I didn't realize was my work wasn't done. The light could well have been in the right place, but it was controlling the light and taking it away from the places I didn't want it, where the craft really came into its own.

The tools you use to control your light are flags and nets. Both come in various shapes and sizes, but they are excellent pieces of equipment to mold and craft the light in your scene. Spill from light sources can leak and spread out, inadvertently lighting up the white reflective wall behind it and upping the level of ambient light. The simple use of a flag to block the light hitting the wall will make sure your light is only going onto your subject. In some very simple scenes you may have an array of flags and nets blocking and cutting down on lights just to give you the image you're after.

Whereas a flag is a solid black cloth material to cut all the light out, a net is a similar shape of a thinner material to help cut back only some of the light. They come in various strengths and sizes to suit whatever your needs might be.

3.78 A net placed in front of a light to help reduce light

3.79 Flags in action to help remove light from unwanted areas

See the photos below for some flags in action. The picture on the left shows the image without any flags, and the picture on the right shows the controlled and flagged frame. Notice how the hotspot and reflections on the cooker behind our actor have been eliminated, and how the background is now darker too.

3.80 Using no flags, light spills over the background, and causes hot spots

3.81 Using flags, the light is reduced from the background and the hot spots are eliminated

Flags and nets are normally held in place by C-stands and arms so you can position the flag in the exact place you need it.

USING THE CLAPPERBOARD / SLATE

The clapperboard or slate is perhaps the most iconic piece of gear in the film industry, but what is it and how do we use it properly? The clapperboard displays all the important information regarding the shot about to be filmed: the title of the film or episode; director; director of photography / camera operator; scene number; shot number; take number; date; roll or card number; and whether the shot is day or night. If Shot 1 is the master shot of the scene, on the first take the board would read Shot 1, Take 1. If we went for a second take, it would read Shot 1, Take 2, and so on. When the shot changes to a new setup, either in angle or lens size, then the shot number and take will change. So the actor's close-up after the master shot had been filmed would read Shot 2, Take 1. The clapperboard's other main function is to provide a visual indication for syncing the sound with the picture, so when the editor is syncing up the pictures with the sound, they can cue up the "clap" from the clapperboard with the "clap" on the soundtrack, and everything will run together smoothly.

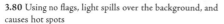

When the camera and sound departments are both recording (i.e., "up to speed"), the clapperboard is placed in front of the camera to mark the take. If the take has people or objects that require sync sound, the clapper is placed upright and marked accordingly, as in the picture below.

3.82 The clapperboard ready to mark a take with sync sound

If the take is silent and contains no sync sound, the camera assistant will either label the clapperboard with the term "MOS" or hold the clapperboard with their fingers between the markers to inform the editor that the take is silent since clapping is impossible. No one really knows the origins of the term MOS, but

3.83 MOS! The clapperboard with the assistant's hand preventing the clap

plausible explanations from the early days of film are "Minus Optical Sound" or "Motor Only Sync."

On some occasions it might be impossible for the clapperboard to be present at the front of the take. Perhaps the shot is too tight on the subject, or there are time considerations. On this occasion the camera assistant would call out "End board" or "Tail slate" to let the crew and editor know the clapper will appear at the end of the take. When it is held in front of the lens after the take, it is placed upside-down to show the editor that the clapperboard information refers to the take beforehand, not the one coming. If you placed it upright, like a normal sync shot, they might assume the clapperboard refers to the shot following the clap. Once clapped upside-down, bring the board upright again to show the editor the information clearly.

3.84 The clapperboard held upside-down to show the editor that this slate refers to the previous take

Other information that would appear on the clapperboard might be the following:

AFS — After False Start. Maybe the camera began recording but had to stop before "action" was called. To let the editor know there isn't a missing take, the assistant labels the clapperboard "Take 3 AFS."

P/UP — Pick up. Perhaps you filmed a good take, but the director would like to just pick up the last two lines or the actor's walk away. Again, so the editor doesn't think they're missing anything, the clapperboard will read "Take 2 P/UP."

SER — Series. If the director would like to roll continuously without cutting, adding SER to the take number lets the editor know there are many takes in this particular clip.

R1 — I've seen this a few times, where directors like to shoot rehearsals. Focus marks and blocking haven't been properly measured, probably due to time, so camera assistants put an "R" before the take number to let the editor and anybody viewing the rushes know it is a rehearsal being shot. If the focus or operating isn't spot on, at least people know the reason for it.

Roll No. — Roll Number refers to the card, tape, or film reel in the camera. Camera assistants place a piece of tape over the camera card slot with the roll information on it; the matching tag also appears on the clapperboard. Once that roll has been used up, the tape is removed and placed on the cardholder to identify the card.

3.85 The clapperboard with the roll number clearly visible

3.86 The camera card slots with the roll number on sticky tape ready to be attached to the cardholder

CONCLUSION

There is a lot of information jammed into this chapter. Some of the technical aspects may take a while to click and make sense, but keep reading and testing these methods and ideas on set. Visit a camera- or lighting-rental company and ask to play with some of the equipment mentioned here. With cinematography, the best way to learn is by doing, so grab some gear, get shooting, see what results you get, and then go back and try again. That "eureka" moment will happen; your confidence will grow, and you'll be on your way to being a better shooter.

CHAPTER 4

Sound

"I asked the sound editor to play one scene in complete silence. When he did, I heard the buzz of a fly. 'I thought we'd agreed that this scene was silent?' I said. He replied, 'Sidney, if you can hear a fly, then the place is really quiet.'"

— SIDNEY LUMET, DIRECTOR

I have asked students in classes and workshops before, "What's more important: sound or picture?" The answers that come back are very interesting. Sound is 50% of the film, after all, and obviously both are used to tell the story. Here are a few perspectives from which we can look at this question: If the picture disappears during a film, people don't mind. They may even think it's part of the story. But if the sound goes, people are immediately taken out of the film and their viewing experience. Film is a visual medium, and if you can tell the story visually with the sound turned off, you're in a good place. Conversely, sound and music stir your emotions; it's the sound effects in a horror movie that make you jump, and it's that subtle crack in an actor's voice as they deliver a heartfelt line that brings a tear to the eye. On a practical front, maybe the sun is going down and you have 20 seconds to get a shot, and the sound recordist needs a few minutes to find a good spot for the boom or hook up a radio mic. In this instance you would shoot the shot without sound as that can be added later, but the picture can't. That's one scenario that you might find yourself in, but not if things had been better planned. But this is filmmaking, and these things do happen. So, overall, both are equally important. However, I would say on a set, when it comes down to the wire, the picture takes priority.

Sound is for the picture. It's not sound for its own sake or a standalone piece of music. The sound must be appropriate for the picture being shot. Poor sound is a big sign of a low-budget project. People are prepared to watch shaky camera work, overexposed hot spots of light, and a few dodgy edits — but if they can't hear what is being said, they don't like it.

A FEW PERSONAL EXPERIENCES

Sound has tripped me up a few times over the years, especially in those early productions when I might have been taking on that role myself as well as operating the camera. I cannot stress this enough: If you can't afford a sound recordist, read up on all the camera and sound settings on your camera and recording gear. I once did not know the difference between the sound-input camera settings very well. What distinguished MIC, MIC ATT, and LINE? I shot a whole scene once with the microphone input on the wrong setting, reducing the sound level by 20 decibels! You would use this setting if you're filming something loud like a live musical performance, but it's not supposed to be used for intimate drama scenes with dialogue. I had the headphones turned right up to hear it, and I thought everything was fine until I played the tapes back! A few sleepless nights later, I managed to get my head around it. What good could come from this experience? I reframed this to determine the correct setting, and I also had my first experience in the world of ADR (Automated Dialogue Replacement) and how time consuming it can be.

Like all of the elements involved in filmmaking, you do the best you can with what you have at the time. A set is fast and compromises need to be made.

WORKING WITH ACTORS

Whether you are a camera operator or a sound recordist, ask the director if you can talk to the talent. This isn't about ego, but maintaining a singular point of view. I've had sound recordists ask actors to put a pause in between lines or to not overlap their delivery. This might contradict the director's instructions, so now the actor is getting flustered not knowing who to listen to. A quiet word with the director to determine what the actor can be asked to do or just to hear the director's thoughts works best. This way the issue is raised through the correct channels. There is an etiquette operating all the time on any set.

ROLES

On smaller, lower-budget productions the sound recordist and boom operator are often the same person. Sometimes you might find a sound team that works together, and each member can carry out one of the roles.

BOOM OPERATOR:

A boom operator or swinger holds the boom pole with the microphone attached, and it's their job to get the microphone in the best position to record the sound. It's a tough job physically: you're holding the boom pole in the air for long periods of time.

PRODUCTION SOUND RECORDIST / MIXER:

The sound recordist records the sound coming through the microphone at the correct levels and makes sure everything is crisp and clear. They might be monitoring and mixing the levels coming in to make sure what the camera is recording is correct, or they could be recording to their own recording format, be it DAT, hard drive, or compact flashcard.

RECORDING AUDIO AND THE CAMERA

Everything is conspiring to prevent the on-set sound recordist from getting a good, clean, pristine track. There is always something: wind, the next-door neighbor drilling, generators buzzing, airplanes . . . Get what you can with what gear you have during the filming stage.

There are a few ways you can record the sound for your film. You can record directly into the camera via an audio feed, or on a separate audio-recording device and sync it up later . . . or both!

Let's look at a few of the combinations and the pros and cons of each.

RECORDING STRAIGHT INTO THE CAMERA

Depending on your budget, you might have just a boom pole and microphone cabled directly into your camera's XLR sockets, and you can adjust the recording volume on the camera. This way your micro-phone is able to get to places an on-board top microphone on the camera won't. What you're unable to do is adjust the recording levels as quickly as you would when using a sound mixer and monitoring as you go. You would set the levels before you start and give yourself plenty of "headroom" above the recording level so if voices do get louder in the scene, the sound won't distort.

4.1 The microphone plugged directly into the camera

A little step up from that is mixing the sound from the boom / microphone through a portable sound mixer. This way your recordist is able to monitor and adjust sound

4.2 The microphone plugged into a sound mixer before running a feed into the camera

4.3 The microphone plugged into a sound mixer before running a feed into the camera and recording sound files to a portable hard drive, compact flash (CF) card, or comparable storage device

levels, or mix multiple audio channels if need be. This is quicker from an overall production point of view as there is no need to sync sound later in post-production. Anything requiring a fast turnaround would benefit from this approach.

The third setup (as seen in image 4.3) involves the mixer and a feed to the camera as above, but also includes recording the audio to a portable hard drive, compact flash (CF) card, or comparable storage device. This provides backup of your sound files and enables a higher-quality recording if needed during post-production.

RECORDING AUDIO SEPARATELY
FROM THE CAMERA

In this last setup, we are no longer tethered to the camera, and the sound files will have to be synced up in post-production. A guide track from the on-board camera microphone could be used to help syncing here. In this setup the sound quality could be higher by using a higher sampling rate of 24 bit when you mix your sound. Some higher-spec filmmaking cameras, for high-end movies and commercials, have no external XLR inputs for you to transfer your audio-mixer feed to the camera, so this has to be done by post-production syncing. Other cameras do have the inputs, but check with your camera rental company.

Out of all the options above, and if your camera has audio inputs, I would recommend you go with the third one: audio feed being mixed into the camera AND sound being recorded on a hard drive or CF card. For short

4.4 The microphone plugged into a sound mixer and recording sound files to a portable hard drive, compact flash (CF) card, or comparable storage device but without recording to the camera

films, student projects, and low-end micro-budget features, I would recommend this method for a few reasons. First, you have the feed as sync for post later if you wish, so if you weren't feeding to the camera and anything happened to the hard-drive recording of the higher-quality tracks, you still have a usable audio track on the picture. It acts as a guide for syncing the higher quality sound if required, but serves as perfectly functional sound if not. If you ever had any issues with those hard drive or files, it's another variable you have to deal with.

HOW DO WE CAPTURE SOUND?

Shotgun microphones are highly directional, so keep the mic pointed in the right place. Imagine there is a laser beam firing out of the end of the mic, aiming for the actor's mouth. Don't point it at the top of their head or in the "general direction" of their face either. This is where concentration also comes in; the actor could be constantly moving, and your microphone needs to reflect that.

You can also help editors and the post-production sound mixer by ensuring the distance the microphone is from the subject is consistent between the close-up and any other shots. You always want to get the microphone as close to the subject as possible, but you also need to think about the acoustics and the quality of the sounds. By pulling back a little with microphone placement when recording the close-up, you still get the crisp clean sound, but also just a hint of the environment and vocal characteristics similar to the sound recorded on the medium or two shot. Without this, the sound characteristics can jump quite considerably when the editor cuts between the two shots, leading to a lot of work in post. If you are editing and mixing yourself, without access to a post sound workflow's services, all the more reason to match the two shots on the day of shooting.

If the boom pole is handled poorly or fiddled with during a take, the resulting sound can rumble and rustle onto the track. A good boom operator will "palm" the boom pole around and rock into position, as seen in this picture (right), rather than

4.5 The boom pole is palmed to reduce friction and interference

gripping it tightly with their fingers and causing rustling, as seen in this picture (right).

The cable from the microphone needs to be neatly wrapped around the pole so it doesn't swing down into shot or make a noise on the track. Before cameras roll, work with the camera operator to find your "edge of frame." This is so you know where the top of the shot is, and the boom won't dip into it during a take. Once you know what your limits are around the frame, you can find your best working position. It's a good idea to find a good reference point on the back of the set or on the horizon. This way you know where you have to be and what your edge is should you swing away and move back to this position.

Try to keep the boom pole parallel to the floor so that your boom is not angled diagonally across set either. There's a danger here of the boom cutting across the camera frame and coming into view. This is a lot tougher on the

4.6 The boom pole incorrectly gripped, which could cause rustling on the soundtrack

4.7 The boom operator using objects in the environment to help keep track of the edge of the frame

4.8 The boom pole resting on the shoulders of the boom operator

arms, so a trip to the gym might be in the cards! Some boom operators like to rest the boom across their shoulders (as seen above) to help with this move.

GEAR

In the film industry there is sometimes a fascination with technology and how it can solve problems. The kit will only get you so far, and then it's the human experience that takes over and sells it. Whatever devices you're using, the fundamentals are the same, so I won't discuss any particular machines as they may soon be out of date.

SOUND MIXER / RECORDERS

There are many recording devices on the market, and there are lots of companies that make a multichannel, battery-operated portable mixer. Some operate as just a mixer unit for the camera, some are able to output a digital signal to record to an external device / hard drive / card, and some even have solid-state recording drives built in. You can also listen to the sound feed the mixer is receiving coming back from the camera. This "confidence feed" will reassure you that you have the sound required and everything is being recorded.

4.9 A multichannel sound mixer

MICROPHONES

There are many different types of microphones by many different manufacturers, and they all perform various functions. Unfortunately there isn't one microphone that is suitable for all scenarios. Some microphones pick up sounds from all directions; others are very specific and only capture what is directly in front. For drama work you might use a shotgun microphone to record sounds directly in front of it, or use a small radio lapel mic hidden under the actor's costume.

Omnidirectional microphone — "Omni" means "all" or "every." This microphone responds to sound from all directions. It might be useful if you have many people sitting around a table or are recording ambient sounds. It's not particularly useful used on a boom pole as you might capture a lot of unwanted noise too.

Directional microphone — A hypercardioid pattern, which refers to the heart-shaped pattern of sound capture that these microphones use, records what's in front and a little to the sides, but not behind. Hypercardioid mics are a good choice for indoor shoots, especially where there are low ceiling heights or tighter space generally.

Shotgun microphone — A shotgun mic has a tighter pickup pattern than a hypercardioid, and a greater rejection of sound coming from the side. This is especially useful in outdoor applications or in noisy environments. Shotgun mics are placed above or below the source, traditionally at a 45-degree angle.

4.10 A shotgun microphone

Lavalier / Lapel / Radio microphone — A small microphone that clips to clothing for getting in close to the talent. It can be cabled or wireless in the form of a radio mic, which is good if your interviewee or actor is moving about. Radio microphones don't

4.11 A radio mic set consisting of a transmitter and receiver

necessarily capture rich sound like shotgun mics do; they are too close to the source. Radio mics can be hidden to make things look spontaneous; as a small omnidirectional microphone, they can be placed upside down if needs be. A radio mic is attached to a transmitter, which is paired with a receiver that is then attached to the camera or sound mixer.

4.12 Windjammer

WINDJAMMER / BLIMP

A windjammer is a long tube that is placed over the shotgun microphone to pretty much do what its name suggests. It does a good job of filtering out a lot of wind noise that could pass over the exposed microphone. It also protects it on set should you swing it into anything.

4.13 The wind sock

WINDSOCK / FURRY COVER

The windsock slides over the windjammer for extra help in cutting out wind noise.

BOOM POLE

Boom poles come in various lengths and materials, with the most popular poles being made of aluminum and

4.14 Boom pole

carbon fiber. They are able to extend or contract depending on what you are shooting. Three to four meters is a good length for most dramas, but make sure it also contracts to around a meter for tighter shooting spaces.

HEADPHONES

A good pair of headphones is essential to monitor the sound you're getting.

4.15 Headphones

CABLES

Depending on what type of gear you're using, you'll find various types of cables and connection leads. An XLR cable is a balanced professional cable with a 3-pin connection, shielded to prevent interference. It connects the microphone to the mixer and is used to run a feed into the camera (if the camera you're using has XLR inputs).

4.16 XLR cable

RECORDING METERS

Level meters are monitoring tools that give you a visual representation of the audio signal using indicators or needles. Loudness is subjective, but an audio level is an objective measurement of voltage. Your ears are the best tools for mixing. Level meters are good aids as long as the camera / mixer / headphones have all been set up and calibrated correctly. If it sounds right, it is right. There are various types of level meters, and we will look at the two most popular. These can be found on portable sound mixers on set, in edit and sound-mixing suites, or both.

Digital meter — A digital meter is what you will find on your camera or NLE software when you edit. These are peak meters that indicate the highest level of sound that is being input into the system. You have two channels representing a left and right stereo signal. Digital audio levels are quoted in terms of decibels, or dBFS (full scale), and the maximum level recordable on this scale is 0, so any sound will be in minus figures, e.g., -12 dBFS. 0 dBFS is a reference level used in the digital arena, and Full Scale (FS) refers to the maximum level

4.17 Digital meter in action

before the digital audio converter overloads or the sound "clips." We've all heard the distortion when something is recorded or played too loud, so headroom has to be established below 0 dBFS.

PPM — PPM stands for Peak Program Meter. These are dials on older portable SQN sound mixers and in some edit suites that show levels. With PPM devices, two small needles move according to the signal strength. PPM readers are popular, as once the incoming sound has hit its peak and the small needle begins to fall back to the 0 position, it moves slowly enough for the human eye to read the measurement.

4.18 A PPM meter

AUDIO SETTINGS ON THE CAMERA

If you decide to record your sound into the camera, whether as a guide track or as your audio feed, there are a few settings on the camera you should be aware of. Depending on your audio setup, you will have your XLR cable(s) from your sound gear connected to the camera's XLR sockets (Channel 1 and Channel 2), and each socket can be switched to three possible settings.

LINE — For taking a strong line level signal from playback / sound mixer / mixing desk.

MIC — For use with an external microphone or radio microphone setup. A slightly weaker signal than Line; boosting it results in slight noise.

MIC +48v — For condenser microphones that need to be powered by the camera.

Somewhere in the camera menu system (depending on the camera being used) you will find an option to select between Channel 1 or Channel 2. If you have just one source coming

4.19 XLR cables attached to the camera's XLR's sockets

into the camera on a single XLR feed, you can set whether the audio is sent to just one channel (Channel 1) or to both as a stereo track (Channel 1/2). If you have a stereo feed from a sound mixer and are coming in through the LINE setting, you would have this set to Channel 1, so any signals coming into Channel 1 go to Channel 1; signals coming in on Channel 2 go to Channel 2, rather than the same sound from Channel 1 going to both channels. Equally, if you had two different sources of audio coming in, maybe one from a boom microphone and one from a radio mic, you would want to keep each channel separate and independent of each other.

There may also be a setting that enables you to record from either the external sources (EXT) or internal on-board sources (INT). Some cameras have a low-quality on-board fixed microphone that is seen as an internal (INT) source. If you are bringing in an audio source from outside the camera, be it a boom microphone, radio mic setups, or a sound mixer, you would need to tell the camera to record the feed coming from those sources by setting the microphone to EXT.

SETTING SOUND LEVELS

Somewhere on your camera, you will find the audio level dials. There will be two dials for your left and right channels. You can use these to set the level of your incoming sound source. Ask the sound recordist to generate a 1 kHz tone signal (a long, uninterrupted pinging noise) from their mixer to help set your dials to a level of -18 dBFS on the camera's digital meters. This way all the sound recorded during the rest of the shoot will be at a solid level, with plenty of head-room for louder moments, and the

4.20 Audio level dials on the camera

mixer and camera aligned via consistent recording levels. Meters at both ends are used to give a visual representation of this 1 kHz tone level. On analog systems using PPM meters, this would be shown as PPM 4.

Good audio levels for dialogue would be between -20 and -12 dBFS on the camera's digital meters, or PPM 4/5 on the SQN mixer meters. You then have from -12 to -6 and just above if anything sudden and loud should happen. On most mixers and recording devices, you also have a limiter switch that will kick in if the sound suddenly peaks past 0 dBFS. Use the levels and your headphones to monitor the sound inputs. When the director rehearses the scene with the actors, this is a good time to set levels and time any movements that might be required.

CHAPTER 5

Directing, Part 1 – The Camera

"Directing is almost like keeping four balls in the air on a monocycle with a train approaching behind you."

— GUILLERMO DEL TORO, DIRECTOR

So what is directing? What are your responsibilities? How do you "direct"?

Directing covers working with the actors on the set, talking about what they're doing and how, and using the camera to help tell your story and bring your "vision" to the screen. A director works with the crew, particularly the director of photography, to find the best possible shots to film the action. It is also a good start to have an understanding of cameras and lenses. As a director you need a strong vision and an overview of what the whole piece is. The entire project should be in your head in one shape or form in order for you to maintain the tone, pace, and feel of the film. Directing is also the ability to be able to think in cuts. How do you see the scene edited together? How can you possibly make decisions or answer questions on what to see or where to shoot if you don't know if it will fit in the finished film? Basically, directing is about knowing what you want.

All of the examples that follow I learned the hard way and the best way, through experience. I've sat in an edit suite cursing myself for missing a shot, or realized I never shot the wide / master of a whole scene so am now without a shot of a character walking away.

ATTITUDE AND APPROACH

Perhaps one of the most important parts of directing is tone. Once the tone of the film has been decided, this can help answer a lot of questions that may come your way. Tone is something that will come to you as you read the script: the pace, the feel, the style. In pre-production and during the shoot, if the costume department, set designer, cameraman, or actor come to you with a question, knowing the tone of the film will help you answer it. If you know the tone, you know how fast to move the dolly or how dark that scene should be. It helps you make decisions on camera style, or even down the line for the grade in post-production. If you work on this and nail it down early on, it paves the way for other aspects to find their place. Tone tells me things like my opening shot and what the music is like. It sets the pace and lets the audience know what they're watching.

Here's a good quote to remember:

"Let the emotion of the scene direct your direction."

— Director Joe Wright

Once you come at it from this position, everything falls into place. So if you have a slow intimate scene of an old man visiting the grave of his recently departed wife, and he gently walks to the headstone, lays flowers, and takes a moment before slowly walking away, is there any radical approach required here? It's probably going to be a quiet and graceful sequence, so you can rule out handheld whip pans and Dutch angles. You don't need a close-up of his feet as he walks in the grass. No handheld over-the-shoulder shots as we follow him in. More than likely, it will be a long, slow dolly move or a static shot on a wide to show he's alone, and then a close-up on his face to see the emotion he's feeling.

Filmmaking usually means shooting scenes out of order. First on the schedule might be the last scene of the film. The next could be Scene 14, followed by Scene 2. So in order for you to judge the tone and pace, and to help your actors, you have to know where you are in the story emotionally and technically at any given time.

CONFIDENCE

Confidence plays a big part in directing, and like most things you need to find a balance. Too confident and you're unapproachable, and the crew will dislike you very quickly. You find yourself being closed to suggestions, as your approach is the one and only avenue. A lack of confidence, and you're a pushover and every crew member suggests things left, right, and center. You try to accommodate and please everyone, and what you end up with in the edit is a mess. It's a fine line. Someone might suggest a better shot or idea than yours. If it works, should you go with it? Of course! Why use your (lesser) idea and dismiss theirs just to remind people you are the director? You are still the person in control of the creative process.

The key to confidence is to be prepared, which we'll address next. Remember, there will always be moments when self-doubt kicks in. You'll question if you can do it, if you can pull it off, and you'll convince yourself that everyone will hate your film. Director Steven Spielberg said something that has always stuck with me: "There is a moment in every film when you think you've got the biggest hit of the century, and other moments when you're going to walk away embarrassed from this. Those feelings can exist within an hour of each other, or a day, or are pulling and pushing you in the editing process."

Self-doubt happens to us all. The trick is to not to let it stop you.

PREPARATION –
SHOT LISTS AND STORYBOARDS

Three keywords for success: preparation, preparation, preparation. Finding what works for you in this area is important. You may write shot lists, draw storyboards, or both, but whatever you do, find what you like and stick with that. A shot list comprises of all the shots you'd like to get done in that day's shooting. It might look something like this:

1. Wide dinner table
2. Medium Dad
3. Medium Mom
4. 2 shot of little Jonny and Susie
5. Close-up food on Jonny's plate as it flies off the table
6. Medium on dog as he eats food off the floor

So there you have a shot list for our little scene. I think it covers the shots we need to tell the story.

Now, the trick here is to not overcomplicate things. I've also seen shot lists like this:

1. Wide of Dad at the dinner table up to the line "Jonny, eat your greens, boy"
2. Shot of Jonny turning to Dad
3. Wide of Dad at the dinner table as he says, "Come on now," turns to mother, and smiles at her before resuming eating dinner
4. Shot on mother as she watches Susie eat her sausages . . .

The difference here is that this shot list isn't written as shots or individual setups of the camera, but as how the director sees it playing in the edit. Shots 1 and 3 are the same camera setup. So the DP might look at this list at a glance and think they have more shots to light than they do. There is also too much information listed. Unless it is a special situation, dialogue is covered in the script. For basic shot lists, it helps things if the list is concise and brief. You need to be able to glance at it and get the information quickly, not have to read lines and lines of superfluous information. Then, as you shoot, you cross off the shots as you go.

STORYBOARDS

Storyboards are little pictures showing the action, much like a comic book. They might look like this image:

| Scene | 11 | Shot | 11.2 | Detail | EXT. BULKHEAD ABOVE BEACH - DAY |

CU on ARTHUR (seated), wide angle lens. His face appears distorted as he fights the itching.

5.1 An example of a storyboard

You don't have to be a fantastic artist to draw storyboards; stickmen will suffice! Some directors use storyboards and some don't, and both have their reasons. Some don't even use shot lists and just wing it, doing whatever they feel. Filming scenes can be complex, even simple ones, and you don't want to find yourself missing important shots to help tell your story. For every director who champions storyboarding everything in the film, you'll find one that doesn't like doing it. Some directors claim it hinders their instincts when on set. Both are right in their own way, but the trick is to find *your* way.

I like to use shot lists for every scene, and then storyboard anything that involves other departments such as visual or practical effects. The special-effects people need to know what shots you're planning so they can prepare for their work. With visual effects / CGI work, that department needs to know what shots are live action and what is green screen in order to make the required elements bring the scene together. Having a storyboard keeps everyone on the same page.

COVERAGE –

HOW TO "COVER" OR SHOOT A SCENE

This is probably the biggest and most important aspect of directing. Tattoo this on the inside of your eyelids:

Coverage is KING.

What exactly is coverage? Coverage is how you plan on filming the scene before you. How are you going to stage it? With what shots? From where?

Once you realize that everything you are doing is about the edit, then you are on your way to a better understanding of what material you need on set. Filming traditional coverage has been the standard approach in Hollywood since movies began.

Some filmmakers disagree with the notion of coverage, and prefer to call it "dump truck directing": shooting everything with no idea how it might come together. I disagree with this. With coverage, you can still use your shots the way you intended, but if a better idea comes late in the edit, you have the additional shots to put the scene together in a different way. Another benefit of coverage is the ability to cut a scene down if your film is running a little long, either for your own sensibilities or to fit a broadcast transmission. If your scenes are all single shots, then you are stuck with those shots and their length can't change.

So let's look at a scenario of two people talking in a room. For this coverage the approach could be:

- Master / Wide
- Single shot character A
- Single shot character B

Or commonly referred to as "Master, Single, Single." This is the foundation which you can then build upon and tweak to your heart's content. This approach is different to shooting wide, medium, or close-up of all action. Shooting every scene like this would be dump-truck directing; you're just collecting footage. Coverage is knowing how you want the scene to look and giving yourself options. Start with this and then add or subtract accordingly.

Let's make our example a couple in a coffee shop. The scene involves a girl breaking up with her boyfriend. So we have a master / wide of the couple on a sofa or at a table to give us a sense of place, and then we can shoot two single angles of each of the characters. Now of course this is just how you are going to film the scene; you might edit this together in any number of ways. The two single shots could be two medium shots, medium close-ups, or close-ups. That's a decision you and your cameraperson make.

So your shot list might look like this:

Wide coffee shop
Medium boyfriend
Medium girlfriend

5.1a A wide shot of our coffee shop

5.1b The first single: Medium shot on the boyfriend

5.1c The second single: Medium shot on the girlfriend

As the scene is about her breaking up with him, you might want to be in tighter on their faces when she breaks the news to convey the emotion. So you could add two close-ups to the list, too:

Wide coffee shop
Medium boyfriend
Close-up boyfriend
Medium girlfriend
Close-up girlfriend

If time is of the essence, you might settle for the two singles being two medium close-ups. Maybe at the end the girlfriend hands back a set of house keys. The wide shot wouldn't show this detail, and in the medium singles they could be out of frame, so now we add another shot to our list:

Wide coffee shop
Medium boyfriend
Close-up boyfriend
Medium girlfriend
Close-up girlfriend
Insert close-up of keys being handed over

As the girl leaves, he watches her go and so we might have a wide of that from his point of view. So we add that to the list. This could be considered a nice add-on and isn't essential, but you could shoot it if you had time. (This extra wide shot is in a different direction to the first wide view, so wouldn't use the same setup.) So now we have:

Wide coffee shop
Medium boyfriend
Close-up boyfriend
Medium girlfriend
Close-up girlfriend

Insert close-up of keys being handed over
Wide of girl leaving coffee shop

So how much of this coffee-shop scene do we film from each of our setups? Inserts aside, you'd film all of it from top to bottom. So if the scene lasts four pages, each wide and single angle would contain the whole four pages of the scene. This way you have the scene covered. If you are in the edit and wonder what the boy's reaction is when she says she's leaving, you can bring up his angle and find it. You might want to edit the scene so you play 80% of it with one character just listening to the other. It's all about their reactions. If you don't film this, then you can't use it. Obviously it's good to use common sense, too: If you are just filming the keys going on the table or being handed over, you don't need four pages of empty hands as we wait for the keys to appear . . .

There are different approaches to coverage. Cinematographer Roger Deakins was interviewed for *American Cinematographer* magazine about his work on *The Village* (2004), directed by M. Night Shyamalan. They shot a wide of two people walking and talking before the characters stopped and finished their conversation. The only coverage they shot was this wide. Deakins asked about shooting singles, but Shyamalan declined, as that was the way he wanted to play it in the edit. "Night definitely has a different idea about shooting, and it's very minimalist," observed Deakins. "Often we weren't even in front of an actor when he or she was talking, and sometimes you don't even see the actor who's talking." Director

5.2 *The Village*

Shyamalan adds, "I don't do traditional coverage per se, where meanings and statements are created in the editing. With that method, the personality of a scene, sequence, and ultimately the whole movie is often decided and / or found much later on. That certainly works for many filmmakers, but it's just not my thing." Watch the movie, and at 11 minutes in you see an example of this. This is a very confident and ballsy approach. Be sure that this is how you want the material to play out, as there is no turning back other than a reshoot!

You could alter our coffee-shop scenario and film a wide, slowly pushing into a two shot and adding an insert of the keys. This way, there is only one way this scene can play. After blocking the scene with the actors and conferring with your cameraperson, you may find that the scene plays perfectly well in the wider shot. You could just go with that.

So what happens if there are more than two people in the scene? Then things get more involved. If the coverage for the scene mentioned in the coffee shop was Master, Single, Single, we now have Master, Single, Single, Single. In *Lord of the Rings* and *Harry Potter*, where some scenes have seven or eight people sitting around a table, the shoots can go on for a week or more to get all necessary coverage. You can be slightly economical in your approach; it's good filmmaking to do so. Perhaps two of the three people are related or married. You might consider turning this extra single shot into a two shot to help show the audience they are related in some way. This way you might not need that extra shot since you've just turned two single setups into one. Your choice of shot size can really help you tell your story and decide on what coverage you need.

Let's look at another example of how your camera coverage could help tell your story. Say we have the girlfriend, her boyfriend, and now the boyfriend's best friend having coffee. So our coverage becomes:

Wide coffee shop
Medium girlfriend
Medium boyfriend
Medium boyfriend's friend

This could change to:

Wide coffee shop
Two shot boyfriend and girlfriend
Medium boyfriend's friend

The two shot saves us time and illustrates the couple's connection. However . . . what if we switched the two shot to the girlfriend and the best friend? And let the single be the boyfriend? How does the audience feel now? If we were to discover that the girlfriend and the friend were having an affair later on in the film, then we wouldn't be surprised.

Out of the Master, Single, Single, which shot should we film first, and why? In 99% of cases, you should film the master first, for a number of reasons. First, it helps the actors and audience orient themselves. We all know where everything and everyone is. In addition, if the camera breaks down, or a catastrophe happens and you can no longer shoot the singles coverage, you have the whole scene in the can. If you started with one of the singles and had to stop for any reason, you only have half the scene. Shooting the wide also serves as another rehearsal of sorts before coming in for the close-up work. Like most things, there are exceptions. The scene might be emotionally heavy for one of the actors and that requires a lot of work. If they are ready to shoot that emotionally demanding scene right away, you should act upon that first. Getting the master out the way for a couple of takes might mean you lose the opportunity to capture them at their best in a single.

A note on the single shots: Each single should ideally match the reverse — this means match the shot size and equivalent position too. If the first single is a medium shot and about 20° off the axis of the character's eyelines, then the other character's single should be the same. Cutting from a medium to a close-up and back to a medium, or shooting Character A in profile and Character B front on, can look very jarring. To make sure the audience's focus is on story and dialogue, avoid this or you risk disorienting and confusing them. It's okay to cut to a different size frame during the scene, but once you cut from a medium to a close-up on one character it's best to match that on the other character too. Take a look at these shots from *Die Hard With a Vengeance* (1995). The medium shots match each other, as do the following close-ups on each character.

5.3 Medium over-the-shoulder shot of Bruce Willis

5.4 A matching medium over-the-shoulder shot of Samuel L. Jackson

5.5 Moving closer . . . a close-up of Bruce Willis

5.6 A matching close-up of Samuel L. Jackson

Now let's shake it up a bit. As noted, use traditional coverage as a foundation. You can adjust and adapt this any way you please. In our coffee-shop scenario, you could start your master on a dolly and slowly push into the medium of the girlfriend. Then all you need is the reverse medium single on the boyfriend. You've just lost one shot from your shot list, and you're now ahead on time. But what have you lost editorially? You don't have a wide of the whole scene for the edit. What if you reached the edit and asked, *What does the wide look like when the girlfriend walks away?* You don't have a full single on the girlfriend, or a close-up / medium of her from the start of the scene. You could shoot your moving master, push into the single, AND shoot the wide again from a static position AND shoot one full single on the girl — but this will obviously add to your shot list and time shooting.

You must be extremely confident how you want to play a scene if you decide to drop coverage and shoot only what you want. From experience, though, your personal taste and thoughts on the scene might change later, come the edit. Your editor might also come up with a wonderful suggestion to cut the scene differently, but you haven't got the material to edit it that way because you didn't shoot it.

CHARACTERS LOOKING AT "SOMETHING"

Showing the audience that a character is looking at or has seen something or someone can be executed in a variety of ways. Most traditionally, you would have what I call a 3-shot montage: a medium or close-up of your character, followed by the point of view (POV) of the person or object they are looking at, and then a cut back to the character. This is sometimes referred to as "reverse angle shooting" or "shot / reverse shot." However, labeling it this way doesn't account for the third shot back on the person looking. Their POV might consist of a wide, medium, or close-up, depending on where they are situated in relation to what they are looking at. Look at the example on the next page of this character looking at their phone.

5.7 A shot of a man looking . . .

5.8 A close-up on what he is looking at

5.9 Cutting back to the man again completes the sequence

This sequence would consist of two setups: one of the person and the other of the object. The editing splits it up into three shots. It might be necessary to use the technique a few times to not only show what they are looking at, but also to convey any distance involved. For example, what if we had a teacher walk into a class looking for a particular student? We might see a close-up of the teacher, followed by the student, then a cut back to the teacher again. However, this series of shots wouldn't communicate that there is a whole class of students present, and that the teacher was looking for a particular one; the editing suggests they found them right away. So we might add a few more shots. We could have a wide of the teacher walking in, a close-up of the teacher followed by a wide of the class (teacher's POV) and a shot of the teacher looking more intensely, then a close-up on the student they're looking for (teacher's POV) before finally ending on the teacher again. Look at the examples below:

5.10 Wide of the classroom as the teacher enters . . .

5.11 A single shot of our teacher looking . . .

5.12 An over-the-shoulder reverse angle reveals the class . . .

5.13 A tighter single of the teacher, tilting his head to get a closer look . . .

5.14 A close-up on the student . . .

5.15 Back to the single shot of the teacher, who's found the student he was looking for . . .

To help connect the POV shot with the person looking, you could use an over-the-shoulder (OTS) to show without a shadow of doubt that they are looking at that person or object. Using the OTS technique also helps convey distance as it gives us some foreground action to help us get our bearings. It's good to see the POV through their eyes, so ideally the POV shot needs to be preceded by a shot of their eyes, either in a medium or close-up shot to really tie the two shots together. A POV shot after a wide doesn't quite work, and sometimes could look like two unrelated shots. Cutting to a close-up of what someone is looking at after a wide shot of them introduces an element of confusion, especially in fast-paced sequences where orientation is paramount.

So, the 3-shot montage is the traditional approach; it's used the world over and works very well. However, if you can find a dynamic way to keep your shots and edits interesting, then you could try something different. Maybe you have a character sitting in a car or looking out of a window. You might see them looking at something, but instead of cutting to a new shot of what they are looking at, you could frame what they are looking at in the reflection of the window and then pull focus from them to the reflection. This not only saves you a shot, but is a little more interesting for the audience.

CUTTING IN YOUR HEAD

Some filmmakers might differ on this approach, but I think it's imperative. When you read a script, you have a vision of the scene playing out; it's simply about going out and getting those shots. Around your shots you give yourself some "handles" and leeway on what is being covered, but you must have a good idea of how the scene will come together. By doing this, you gain confidence as a director to know whether you have a scene in the can or need to go again for another take. If directors don't know what they want, they'll keep shooting every angle until every line is perfect, just in case they might need it in the edit. If you find yourself shooting an emotionally heavy scene with two characters who start arguing, you might start with the wide and find the delivery of a line or two isn't completely as you'd like. However, time is pressing to get everything shot; come the edit, you know you'll be in tighter on a medium or close-up shot to reflect the growing intensity of the scene. This gives you the confidence to move on from the wide to the singles. You don't need word-perfect performance on every line on every take. If you're insecure about how something will come together you might keep shooting, eating into the rest of your shooting day.

Director Alfred Hitchcock had a good notion he used in most of his films come the edit where he'd cut from the wide angle to the singles when a scene's emotional intensity went up a gear. So when our girlfriend enters the coffee shop and makes chitchat about what drinks she's ordering and how she had trouble parking nearby, this could play on the wide or the two shot. But when she brings up leaving the boyfriend, the single close-up or medium might be preferable.

If you decide to shoot your scene in one shot, how could you continue this notion of shifting gears during a scene like Hitchcock did? You could signify the shift in tone or mood of the scene with a camera move. Director of photography Eduardo Serra, A.F.C. and director M. Night Shyamalan achieve this in their film *Unbreakable* (2000). A scene sees actors Bruce Willis and Robin Wright at a bar on a wide shot. They are having a date night to rekindle their romance, and the dialogue is flirty and fairly light. When the conversation changes to Robin Wright asking when Bruce Willis's character thought their relationship wouldn't last, the camera begins a very slow push in from a wide to a two shot, signifying the shift in gears.

5.16 *Unbreakable*

GIVE THE CHARACTERS SOMETHING TO DO

Having the characters performing an action as they talk is a great opportunity to reveal character through action. Maybe in an office, the printer isn't working and one character is trying to unplug it or change the ink cartridge. Maybe they're at home unsuccessfully cooking an elaborate meal, or working on a car engine? The point being, giving the characters a piece of business or action within the scene can help elevate it. It also opens the door to possible subtext opportunities and can make the characters seem more rounded or fallible. The task at hand might be related to the story, or it might just be something irrelevant, but it can be a wonderful opportunity to make the scene more interesting. Mixing the two could be a good chance to plant an object or device in front of the audience that at the time might seem irrelevant, but could be very useful come the end of the film.

If a character has something else to do (mix cooking ingredients, hammer a nail, eat food, or repair a computer), it allows for physical actions that can then be interrupted. If the dialogue in the scene generates a reaction, stopping their physical activity can reflect this visually and reveal something about the characters.

STAGING AND ORIENTATION –
PLACEMENT OF YOUR ACTORS AND HAVING THE ACTION MAKE SENSE TO THE AUDIENCE

How you stage your scene with your actors, and where you put the camera, are the other big secrets to having your film look the best it can. You can shoot on the highest format you can find, with the best locations possible, but if you don't stage it and film it right, it is all a waste of time. There is a keyword that I discovered late in the game which unlocked it all for me: DEPTH.

When you stage and compose your shots using depth, you are able to tell your story better and faster; you might need fewer shots to do so. Depth is having more information available about the location in the frame. Depth shows you more detail in the background and places your actors better in their surroundings.

A good example might be filming in a corridor where two people stop and talk to each other. If you positioned your actors facing each other across the corridor, as seen in Diagram A, and shot your coverage, you'd get nothing but white walls over their shoulders. However, if you staged the scene as per Diagram B, with their backs to the corridor, you're able to show the depth of the location and remind the audience where they are with each shot. Aesthetically, too, you have so much more going on in the image. The wide shot of them talking would look good, with the two people in the corridor, but it's about getting their positions right in this wide that sets you up well for the singles.

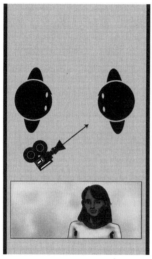
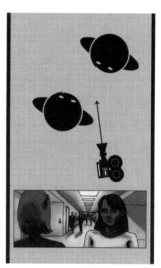

5.17 Shooting across the corridor gives no depth to the shot and isn't visually interesting

5.18 Shooting down the length of the corridor offers you depth and makes for a more interesting shot

Filmmaker and lecturer Alexander Mackendrick (*Sweet Smell of Success*) in his book *On Filmmaking* (look it up and go buy it) gives the best description of how to achieve a great-looking shot by staging in depth. Whatever room or location you find yourself filming in, find the long axis of the room by drawing a line across from one corner to the opposite corner, as seen in the following picture:

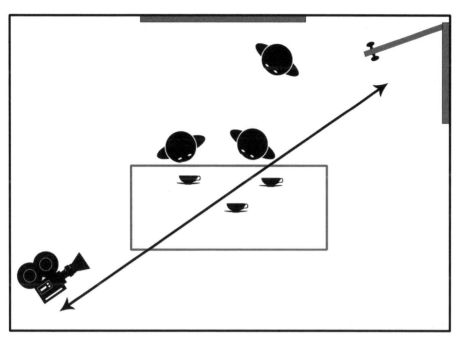

5.19 Finding the long axis of the room gives you more depth to your shots at any location

The best places to position your actors and your camera are anywhere along that line. You might have a gorgeous-looking, expensive location, but if you only shoot in the corner of it, the audience will never see it. The problem is the director does see it, but only in their mind's eye. They remember what the location was like when they were shooting and bring those memories to the edit, but the audience isn't privy to that thought process.

Enabling more depth within a shot all starts with the blocking and how you stage the scene. Consider the examples on the next page. Imagine that in this coffee shop, our characters are positioned against the back wall. We could shoot from across the room for the wide, and maybe have some foreground action of customers walking in front of the camera.

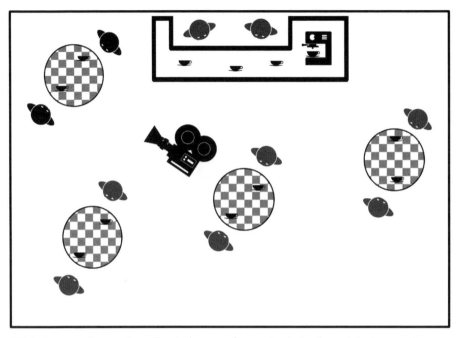

5.20 Staging your action up against walls or in the corner of a room doesn't allow for much depth to your shots

However, what if we positioned the characters in the center of the room? This now enables us to have a sense of depth behind our characters. We can see movement behind as well as in front. The depth of field will be highlighted, allowing us to focus on the actors.

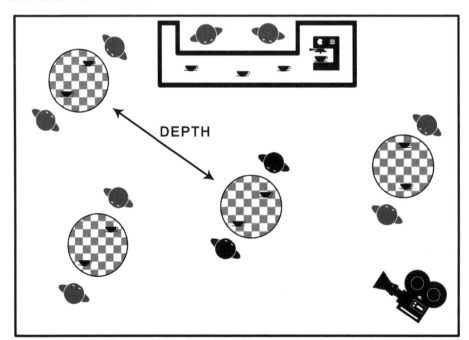

5.21 Staging your action in the center of the location allows for depth and more interesting backgrounds

ORIENTATION

It doesn't matter where people or things are in reality when you film; it's where the audience thinks they are that counts. What does the camera see? Orientation is important to keep in mind when filming and staging. The second the audience is disorientated or confused, you've lost them and it could take a while to get them back.

Wide shots (or masters) are some of the most important shots in your creative toolkit, essential for orientation since we instantly know where people are in relation to each other. Imagine a scene with a family around a dinner table. The father sits down to discuss the son's poor report card. Halfway through the scene, the son stands up to leave before being told to sit back down. A few lines later the mother gets up to collect the report from the kitchen and brings it back to the table. Finally, the scene ends with the son storming off to his bedroom. The wide angle could be used here a number of times. All of the instances where a character stands, leaves, or enters would be an opportunity to cut to the wide to show this information. Not only does it orient the audience and literally let them know what is happening, but it also provides that time for the audience to take a breath before we dive back into the meat of the dialogue. If I was only planning to use the wide shots at those moments, I would still shoot the whole shot as part of the coverage. Knowing when I plan to use it would allow me to let poor line delivery go during the rest of the take. I would also look for moments to use the wide; if there is a tiny camera bump or a poorly operated pan on a key scene of a character leaving or entering, I would capture that moment again.

Action films have a tough job with orientation if it's done poorly. Trying to keep the tension and excitement up is only possible if the audience knows where the hero is in relation to the villain and all other items of importance. Let's say the hero is shooting at the bad guy from across the room and is running out of bullets, but spots a spare gun under the chair ten feet to his right and a doorway he can escape through behind him. First, though, he has to get to the innocent civilian hiding under the table to his left! Phew! How do we show all that in fast, exciting cuts, and make sure the audience knows who's who and where everyone is? It's important to have that "third eye" that is able to see what the audience will see. Knowing where everyone was when you filmed it is not sufficient justification for just filming mediums or close-ups and hoping the audience sees it the same way.

One of the best examples of this type of staging is in the finale to the film *Robin Hood: Prince of Thieves* (1991; director, Kevin Reynolds). This action-packed scene sees Robin (Kevin Costner) attempt to rescue his merry men from being hanged in the castle grounds in front of the villainous Sheriff of Nottingham and rich barons. In the audience of peasants are some of Robin's friends ready to aid the rescue, with others placed around the castle walls alongside Robin looking down into the courtyard below. It's a large-scale scene and has lots of action. We won't feel the tension build unless we know exactly where everyone is. We need to stay engrossed and not get confused, or the scene won't work dramatically. The secret to keeping this orientation is in the use of a few simple shot sizes and techniques. Editing obviously plays a crucial part in telling the story and tying it all together, but it's the shots themselves that do the work. Robin and his men are established in their surroundings through the use of wide shots, over-the-shoulder (OTS) angles, and by framing foreground elements in other shots too. Having a close-up of Robin Hood, followed by an OTS shot down into the courtyard to see what he is looking at, joins things together. It also creates depth since we have some foreground action going on in the frame. The over-the-shoulder shot, a piece of the frame that anchors us to

5.22 Still from *Robin Hood: Prince of Thieves* showing the over-the-shoulder shot in action, giving us distance and keeping the orientation

the characters and aids orientation, is instrumental in this type of storytelling, enabling us to process the information a lot more quickly. OTS shots can also provide us with another important piece of information: distance. A close-up of someone looking, cutting to a close-up of what they are looking at and then cutting back to the person again, is all good. The grammar of editing tells us they are looking at that object, but how far away is it? Two meters? Ten meters? The over-the-shoulder shot can convey that it's at least across the room, about eight meters away — or whatever it might be. The finale to *Robin Hood* contains all of this, and audiences are never confused as to where characters are in relation to one another.

TELLING THE MINI STORY

Following our coverage and orientation sections, sometimes you need to have a sequence that "tells a story." Not the story of the film as a whole, but a small section that tells its own mini story. It might be that we need to show one character has seen another character witness something, or that someone has muddled the important files before their boss's presentation, or that they've delivered the letter to the wrong door. That "story" is sometimes obvious to us as the reader or director, but the audience needs to understand it. Coverage and the shots you choose will all play a part in making sure this information gets across to the audience. Let's look at another example from the finale of the action-adventure film *Robin Hood: Prince of Thieves* to illustrate this. Robin's friend Little John and his wife watch on as their son and members of their camp are about to be hung from the gallows by the Sheriff of Nottingham. The order is given to the executioner to kick away the stools supporting each of the prisoners, including Little John's teenage boy. Being a large, strong individual, Little John attempts a rescue, charges the wooden gallows, and razes them to the ground. So what shots do director Kevin Reynolds and editor Peter Boyle use to tell the story of "Little John brings down the gallows to rescue the prisoners"? Let's take a look.

5.23 Medium shot establishes that the prisoners are in trouble.

5.24 Medium shot of Little John spotting the gallows and running to the rescue.

5.25 Medium shot of Little John charging the gallows and thrusting into them.

5.26 Close-up on Little John's face to show his strength and pain.

5.27 The boy's anxious mother watches on.

5.28 The all-important wide shot that shows the whole action: Little John against the pillar and the gallows moving, giving us orientation and the results of his efforts.

5.29 Medium shot of Little John and the prisoners in one shot; seeing the action and reaction together.

5.30 Close-up shot of prisoners' legs nearly on the floor — they're almost there!

5.31 Close-up shot of feet landing showing us they're on the ground safe.

5.32 The moving gallows structure hits another wooden panel, preventing it from falling any farther.

5.33 Close-up shot of the prisoners gasping — they survived!

5.34 Close-up shot of Little John's son — he's alive!

5.35 Two shot of father and son reunited.

5.36 Medium shot of the mother looking on, relieved.

Each of these shots tell an important part of that mini story. Not only the practical, physical story, but the emotional one too. The father's pain, the father and son reuniting, and the mother's relief. Each shot had to be the right shot for the right time. If some had been a little closer, it might not have been so clear what was happening. If some shots had been a little wider, it might not have conveyed the excitement and emotional turmoil of the scene. All the shots put together "tell the story," and the sequence is complete.

180-DEGREE RULE OR CROSSING THE LINE

Another aspect to help orientation is the 180-degree rule, also known as "crossing the line." From my years in teaching, this single thing seems to be the one aspect most students get hung up or confused about. They either don't understand it or become overly cautious about it. One thing to remember is filmmakers break it all the time. Sometimes intentionally, sometimes not. The trick is to know when you should obey the rule and when it's okay to break it. The whole point of it is to help keep orientation, but if you find your angle or edit crosses the line and breaks the rule, although your orientation is still intact, then you can let it go.

So what is it? The "line" is an imaginary line that connects two or more people and / or objects. Picture a line running from someone's eyes to where they are looking. A bit like the picture below.

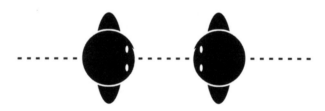

5.37 The "line" drawn between two people or objects

Once we have decided to set up our first angle of the coverage, which will probably be the wide, it is advisable to keep all other camera angles and setups on the same side of the line that has been established from that first wide. See camera placements on the next page:

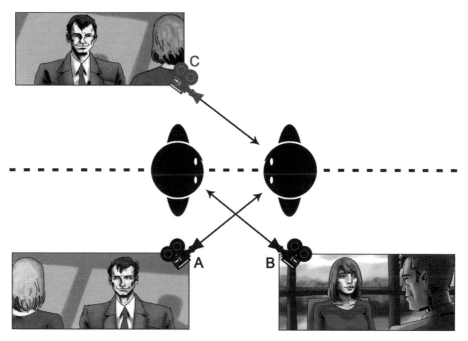

5.38 The images next to the camera positions show us how the shots will make it appear that the two characters are looking the same way if we cross the line and use camera position C

Camera positions A and B are the correct places to film the singles of this scene after the line has been established in the wide shot as seen in the picture above. If, however, you swapped position A out for position C, you would be crossing the line. Remember, it doesn't matter where the characters are in relation to each other or objects when you filmed, it is what the camera sees once the scene has been edited together.

Look at the corresponding images that the camera placements will give us in our picture. The close-up from position B and the close-up from position C give us images that look the same. It appears that the woman is looking in the same direction as the man, even though she is not!

CHANGING EYELINES

Another thing to take into account is that an actor can cross the line for you. "What?" I hear you say. Yeah, this is where you might need to pay extra attention. You may have set up the cameras correctly, but Anna is talking to Simon, and Simon gets up and walks to the door behind the camera. If Anna has been looking from the left of frame to the right during the conversion:

5.39 Anna looks left to right in this first frame

5.40 Simon looks back at Anna from the righthand side of the frame to the left

Then Simon gets up and moves to the door . . .

5.41 Simon gets up and moves to the door

. . . and Anna's eyeline follows him off to the left of the screen . . .

5.42 Anna's eyeline follows him off to the left of the screen

Anna has now changed the line, and the camera will find itself on the other side of it. Simon, when he gets to the door and turns to continue the conversation, will now have to look from the left to the right to match the new line made by Anna's eyeline change.

5.43 Simon now looks from the left to the right to match Anna's eyeline

5.44 Anna now looks from the right to the left of the frame

5.45 Simon's close-up also has him looking from the left to the right of frame

(Left to right, or vice-versa, is described from the camera's point of view. The person is literally looking from the left side of frame to the right.)

Sometimes the line can be reset. If a character leaves frame on the left, and the next time we see them they are walking directly toward us down the center of the frame, then they now are free to walk or look in any direction they please. If they walk or look elsewhere, maintain that newly established direction. Another occasion might be if you leave the character and cut to something else. When you return to your character, you have allowed them to move on or walk into frame from a different side.

CONNOTATIONS –
WHAT DOES THE SHOT MEAN?

Connotation is a great word to remember. A connotation is an associated meaning. Connotations are the origins of thinking a little more abstractly. It helps to think about the meanings behind shots and colors being used in the film. Subtly the audience picks up on these touches, and a little more resonance is infused into the moment.

So ask yourself: "What are the connotations of this shot?" Being able to think this way might help you to decide between two different lenses, or whether to have smoke as diffusion, or whether the actress wears the red coat or not. Stylistically, handheld connotes a point of view or immediacy, or even a slight apprehension. Static shots could mean rigid, boring, quiet, confident. However, you might want to use these connotations to your advantage. The static wide, with its association of nothing happening, might work in your favor if something dramatic is about to happen or someone bursts into a room. Your choice of shot here lulled the audience into a comfortable place and therefore made the surprise even more effective.

One of the best examples of shots and their meaning that I've seen is in the film *The Pledge* (2001), starring Jack Nicholson and directed by Sean Penn. In one scene Nicholson's cop is reluctantly attending his own retirement party. In one wonderful shot, we see Nicholson center frame with the party taking place behind him, and everyone else having fun. Nicholson is out of focus, and the partygoers are all in focus. He simply doesn't fit in here, and the subtle direction and camerawork tell us that. No dialogue required.

5.46 Still from *The Pledge*

Try to find a way of thinking in these slightly abstract terms. They help inform your choices. It's a gut feeling about what things mean beyond their literal sensibilities. Sometimes it may just be an instinctual feeling, and you can't quite put it into words and articulate it just yet. As a director, your job is to hold these feelings and approaches all in your head. When you know your film so well that all the things that work and don't work become obvious, your main job, making decisions, becomes much easier.

One word of caution with shots and their meanings, though. Be careful not to stretch this idea too far. I've witnessed a few directors disappear down the abstract rabbit hole with ideas that will never translate to the audience and only ever mean something to them. A lot of what you might introduce to the frame could work consciously or subconsciously, making the audience feel a certain way without them really knowing why. This is good filmmaking. Having a wide shot to help demonstrate the character's loneliness translates to the screen and to the audience. Having an extra feather in the character's hat to show they secretly want to fly away from their boring life does not.

EMBEDDED INFORMATION –
WHAT DOES THE CAMERA SEE?

Embedded information is when the script contains information that doesn't translate to the screen and the director will find it's simply unshootable. Consider this excerpt:

```
INT. OFFICE — DAY

Jack shuffles into his office to see an envelope on
his desk. He opens it, and a bullet falls out. Jack
realizes that Johnson sent it as a warning to stay
away from Johnson's wife. Jack knows exactly where
Johnson would be about this time. He checks his gun
in the holster and runs out to find him.
```

So what's wrong with that scene? A lot. We have to think about "what the camera will see." The camera sees Jack walk in, open the envelope, see the bullet, check his gun, and run out. The camera doesn't "see" the realization that Johnson sent it, so how does the audience know that information? We also don't know it was sent because of his wife.

Sometimes filmmakers keep half of the film with them in their head when they watch their own work. You have to be able to be more objective and see the whole piece from the audience's point of view; otherwise the film might make sense to you but no one else. When actors read your script, these things might be brought up and questioned, so it's worth taking note if someone flags an issue that is confusing to them. And speaking of working with actors . . .

CHAPTER 6

Directing, Part 2 – Actors

"What's important is not the emotion they're playing,
but the emotion they're trying to conceal."

— SCREENWRITER TED TALLY

Directing actors is a tough one. Every actor will approach each role differently. Some actors don't like to discuss too much, whereas others need guiding through every scene and want to talk about everything. It's your job as director to be a different director to each of your actors. Adapting to each actor's style can be hard, though. Some don't like to rehearse and like minimal takes, whereas others might require multiple takes before they feel the scene works. As a director, you might have both of these actors in the same scene . . .

There is no set approach to directing that everyone must follow, so it's important to find the way that works best for you. What I'll attempt to do is give you a good starting place and a few things you could avoid. The one thing I would stress is that you should do what you want to do, not what you think you *should* do as a director because that's what you think the job involves. An actor would have done all their homework in whatever form that might take before they get to set, and you as a director should also have done yours.

IN REHEARSAL / ON SET

To make your job easier and avoid a lot of unnecessary discussion, the best approach is to first see what the actor brings to the table. How did they see the character or scene? Why spend minutes (or hours!) discussing or telling them what to do, only to discover they were going to do that anyway? No need for discussion then. Allowing them to do their thing first shows trust, which is the most important thing for an actor to have from you. Then all you have to do as a director is nudge them one way or another on the little nuances.

Rehearsal is a good thing. Let's get that out in the open right now. Actors sometimes like to borrow from the old idea of not wanting to rehearse too much so they may "keep it fresh." I've never really understood this notion; it's an actor's *job* to make the material look "fresh" the hundredth time they perform it. If you're well-rehearsed, and a bed of confidence has been laid, this allows for spontaneity. You are then confident and open to new, "fresh" things happening since you know that if they don't work, you can revert back to what worked in rehearsal. If you haven't rehearsed and you try something new and it doesn't work, what have you got left? Stress, nerves, and apprehension. Also, what does that say about theatre work? Theatre shows rehearse for weeks and months before opening night. Does that mean those performances are stale and dull since they've done them so many times before? Confidence is what is at the root of all actors' problems; their job puts them in a vulnerable position. To quote actor Paul Newman when talking about rehearsal, "I don't know why this hasn't caught on . . ."

TALKING TO ACTORS

So what on earth do you say to your actors? How do you discuss things? How can you help them if any guidance is needed? There is a secret here that will make your relationship and time on set go much more smoothly, quickly, and in a way that everyone comes out on top.

That secret is:

Questions.

Questions are the secret when dealing with actors. Form statements as questions on set:

"Steve, what do you think about playing this scene by the window? Does that work for you?"

"Are you okay to play this just on the wide, Lauren?"

"What do you think about not picking up the bag until the third line?"

This way you're not *telling* them what to do, you're *asking* if they can do what you want them to do. And by forming this as a question, you're asking for their input so they feel like they've made some contribution to the outcome of what their character is doing. This works not only because of the way it makes them feel, but also because they could have an excellent comment to make, something you haven't thought of. If you get a funny notion or idea or something from them, follow it. As a director you can of course seek others' input, but then ultimately you make the decision as to what to go with. In any given scene, here is a good question to ask your actor in regard to the other actors in the scene with them.

"What do you want them to do?"

This is also good if you find yourself in a bind. If an actor asks you a question and you don't know the answer right away (this is okay, by the way), you could reply this way. The main question to ask the actor, and what the actor should be asking themselves every moment of their being, is:

WHAT DO YOU WANT?

A character is always wanting for something. Always. Nothing else matters. Even if they get what they're after, their "want" is now replaced with something else. Ultimately it doesn't matter what color tie the character is wearing, what car they drive, or how they like to hold their teacup; what they "want" is the important thing. This is what drives them. The want is the objective. You might hear an actor ask, "What is my objective?" Or the classic, "What is my motivation?" It's the same thing. I'd be a little nervous if an actor asked this, since they obviously hadn't done their homework! However, if they need a little nudging or a reminder, then this is what they're asking for. So the "objective" or "want" is the thing you're always after, but how they play this objective is the key thing.

ACTION VERBS

One useful tool to help an actor play their want or objective is to use action verbs. Action verbs are verbs that express doing something: *Will BEGS forgiveness. Jim QUIZZES his brother.* Once I discovered this, it opened up and clarified so much. You use action verbs to help the actor portray what the character "wants." Action verbs are also a useful tool for an actor if they've been given some confusing direction. Consider this direction to an actor and spot the action verb.

"So your daughter has just walked in the door. Interrogate her until you find out where she's been."

What's the keyword here? "Interrogate." What connotations or associations does this word bring up? For me, I associate it with the police "interrogating" a suspect. Hard, firm, maintained eye contact, in close proximity. Interrogate would be an action verb that focuses and directs the actor. Mixing this up with questions, you could ask the actor, "What are you trying to get him or her to do?" This way they come up with the verb themselves. They could answer, "I'm trying to convince her to marry me." "I'm seducing her." "I'm begging her to give me the money." So what physical and vocal associations do you think about when you hear the verbs used above? For me, "convince" means talking slightly fast, standing a little closer to the person. Seduce means talking softly and slowly, close to the other character. Begging would mean I'm almost on my knees, on the verge of breaking down if I don't get what I want.

As a director, you can break a scene down and find the verbs that correspond with the action. You might find that for the first part of the scene, he's "quizzing" her on where she's been. When she fails to answer, he moves up to "interrogating." When she still refuses to say, he "warns" her of the consequences of not answering. Action verbs allow the actor to play the objective with an emotional center. It is also worth noting that playing a verb forces the actor to focus their attention on the other person in the scene. By doing this, they're never allowing themselves the opportunity to think, "How am I sounding? How am I coming across? Am I doing this right?" This could be good advice for life in general, too. As soon as you focus on others and not on yourself, everything has a way of working out. (Think "What can I buy my wonderful wife for Christmas?" Not "I hope she spends loads on me.")

Here are some great usable action verbs and their possible connotations:

Inform	Cold, straight-talking, no emotion attached.
Attack	Violent, physical, making contact.
Badger	To talk continuously, pulling on someone's arm, poking them as you go.
Intimidate	Standing too close for comfort, not breaking eye contact.
Warn	Firm, controlled, pointing a finger.
Confront	Standing close, in their face, never breaking eye contact.
Lecture	A one-sided conversation wherein one person assumes superior knowledge. A parent lecturing their child about the dangers of staying out late.
Convince	Talking fast, continuous supporting arguments, convincing someone to marry you.
Quiz	Asking a question with no emotion attached. Like a pub quiz or competition.
Interrogate	Asking a question, but like the police or other authority figure. Firm, serious, and demanding an answer.
Beg	On your knees, like a beggar in the street. Talking uninterrupted.
Suffocate	To suck all the air out of a conversation. Nonstop talking and close proximity.
Seduce	To talk softly, making puppy-dog eyes at the object of your advances, moving in close to their personal space.

You can of course really make things come to life by playing their opposites. SEDUCE would be a great verb to play for a husband making his feelings known to his wife after their Valentine's Day meal. But what if an abusive husband "seduced" his wife, whispering in her ear that if she doesn't cook his dinner right, they'll be consequences? That is really scary. Conventional wisdom might suggest playing it in a threatening manner, but by playing the opposite and "seducing" her, you could make it even creepier and add a lot more layers to the scene.

WHAT NOT TO SAY TO ACTORS

"Result direction" is when a director asks for what they want in a literal form: "Say it louder." "Walk faster." "Turn your head on that line . . ." Result direction is considered a no-no and bad practice, but I admit to using it myself on occasion. There are moments when you might need to use result direction. Maybe time is pressing, or you're working with young children. However, result direction usually results in mechanical, contrived movements. Using action verbs helps the actor portray the emotion and "want" of the scene with their body language, delivery, tone, volume, and eye contact, all in the correct proportions to each other, to give a convincing and realistic performance. Result direction breaks these elements apart and treats them separately. "Speak louder, don't look away, point!"

I've also heard directors say, "Give it more oomph!" or "Now give the scene a little something . . ." or "More energy this time. Make it sparkle . . ." If you know what any of these mean, then please let me know. These are generic catch-all directions that don't really mean anything. I've watched actors' faces when they've heard these directions, and they are normally followed by a confused look and more discussion.

BEHAVIOR

As a director, all you are interested in from your actor is their behavior. Remember: What does the camera see? If the camera doesn't see it, it does not exist and things need to be physical in order for the camera to photograph them. So, don't tell your actor what to think or feel; tell them what to do. Unless the actor's homework, thought process, and backstory aids or produces behavioral change in movement or line delivery, it is pretty pointless. All direction from you should result in a behavior of some sort. Intellectual talk should be kept to an absolute minimum. Actors like backstory, and sometimes like to create their own if it's not in the script, but how does this produce behavior? You could ask if it was important to the character and the story, would it not be in the script in one form or another? To create unnecessary weight for the character means more information rolling around the actor's head, stopping them from "being" in the scene and playing what the character "wants."

William Ball in his book *A Sense of Direction* gives a nice, polite way to stop intellectual discussions in rehearsal or on set. He suggests simply saying: "Show me . . ." Asking the actor to show what they mean instead of discussing a move or idea stops discussion and hopefully shows what influence it can have on the scene at hand.

Here's actor Anthony Hopkins on why he likes working with *Hannibal* director Ridley Scott: "He doesn't want to talk about it or pontificate about it or analyze it. [He says,] 'I want you to come through the door and cut his head off. Is that all right? Let's do it.' All the rest and all the hogwash about talking about it and analyzing it is just a waste of time."

Sometimes it's easy to slip into result direction, but try to find a more creative way to get what you want; get that change in behavior and still correspond with the actor's performance. I once directed a wonderful actress in a scene where her character was rummaging through kitchen drawers and had to look up to see the wall clock had stopped. It was a fast scene; she glanced up quickly and could see the clock had stopped, but from an editing standpoint, I needed a little longer on her look to comfortably cut to the shot of the clock. As it stood, her head never stopped moving. Now, "hold the look longer" would be result direction and might have stopped her actions and movements while she consciously waited longer as per my "direction." Besides, how much longer IS longer? So, instead I said, "Make sure the clock is definitely stopped . . ." This direction meant her actions stayed consistent with the movements leading up to it. She made the decision as to what was long enough, and then continued on with the rest of the scene.

EDITING AND ACTING

I think the best-kept secret for an actor is the value of visiting an edit suite. Once you have an idea of how a film is put together, it will inform your approach to the work. I feel that the editing process is so important in shaping a performance that it deserves a mention here. A story is told in cuts, not performance. An actor can be transformed from mediocre to very good by an expert editor using lines from take 1 and take 4, with a look from take 5 and a final goodbye from take 2. The actor might view the finished film and think that it was all done in one shot.

Editing holds the key to how little an actor really has to do. If you're an actor starting out, find an editor or filmmaker and sit in on their editing sessions to see how a scene is constructed. It's better you not sit in on a film with which you're actually involved (the director wouldn't care for it either), but see if you can observe a project a friend is making. I've used editing tricks such as repurposing shots of actors looking down, looking away, or biting their lip that were filmed *after* I'd called cut. And it was a perfect performance for the scene! The camera is still rolling for a few seconds, and it's that moment I've used in the final film. What does this tell us about what the actor needs to be thinking or doing?

Juxtaposition is defined by having two things side by side, in our case two shots. Each individual shot has its own meaning, but when the two are cut together a new, third meaning is created. Lev Kuleshov was a film director in Russia in the 1920s. He demonstrated his theory of montage and juxtaposition by setting up an experiment. He filmed a man in close-up with a neutral expression on his face and then intercut this image with a shot of three different things: a bowl of soup, a cross, and a woman. Audiences were shown these edits of the man, the object, and the man again as three separate sequences, and an intriguing reaction took place. Audiences marveled at the man's look of hunger when they were shown the sequence with the bowl of soup, or the man's sorrow after the sequence with the cross, or the man's romantic feelings when intercut with the woman. His expression never changed, only the shot in between.

It was the editing that made the audience think he was hungry or sorrowful or romantic. Not the performance. It allowed the audience to project whatever feelings they wanted onto the actor's face in the exact degree they wanted. For the actor to "act" any more would result in some cheesy overacting, or "honking and hooting" acting, as Anthony Hopkins calls it. He says, "Stillness and economy are much more effective; you don't need to all pull faces . . ." The trick is to avoid over-emoting and trying to "tell" the audience what they should be feeling. Let the camera and the audience do the work for you, and they'll read whatever they want to into the performance.

All good screen actors know how little they actually have to do. They know the audience will project the exact amount of emotion onto the blank canvas and believe the actor's performance.

CHAPTER 7

Editing

*"It's exciting to see a first cut. It's like giving birth. That
initial Is it a boy or a girl? What do we have?"*

— Pietro Scalia, editor

Editing is one of my favorite parts of the filmmaking process. Everything you
do during production gears up toward the edit. Every little shot, look from
an actor, or insert helps tell the story as the film is made in the edit suite.
Besides the script, performances are another area that can be polished during
the edit. When you've cut a film and you hear a laugh or cry from the audience
at the right moment, it's exhilarating. You've done your job as an editor and as
a director.

Why do we edit? For two reasons. Firstly, for continuity. We need to make
sure actions look real and convincing and that the scene looks like it is unfolding
naturally in front of our eyes. We need smooth cuts as the characters walk up the
path and open the door, or whatever the scene might be, so that we're not jarred
out of the viewing experience. Secondly, we edit for effect. To make the audience
feel a certain emotion, be it joy, terror, relief, or excitement. The editor is juxtaposing images together to help create a feeling.

MY START

My first few films as a kid were shot "in-camera" as we had no editing equipment.
When we pressed the record button, that was the beginning of the shot; when we

pressed stop, that was the cut. So everything had to be shot in continuity and had to be planned ahead of time; there was no going back and changing things. There was no post, no sound effects, no titles, no music added after, and everything had to be played on screen. Music was started and stopped when the camera started and stopped, sound effects were done by friends off camera, and titles were hand-written cardboard sheets pinned to a garden fence. One scene in an action movie we made featured a character in a fight having his face burnt on a hot stove. We had to be inventive here and have his face held to the cold hob close to camera just as an out-of-shot crew member squeezed a wet tissue over a hot hob behind the actor's head. Sound effect accomplished! Our limited technology forced us to be creative, which was an excellent learning tool.

WHERE DO YOU START ON THE FIRST SHOT OF THE EDIT?

Some people can be paralyzed by this. What to put down first? Out of all these takes and shots, what could be the start of the film or scene? Here's the best approach. Put anything down. Start on that wide or whatever and just start cutting. When you first saw the scene in your head, what did you see? Start there. You'll soon get a feel for whether things are working or not. If they are, then keep going; if they're not, then you can go back as you now have something to change. You can't tell what is working and what is not by looking at an empty timeline. Print out a copy of the script, and follow it as you cut; don't go by the shots themselves for guidance. There might be a little look or movement mentioned in the script that you don't notice. You deem it unimportant and cut it out, but the gesture does impact the story. Having the script in front of you can help keep you on track.

I like to start a scene on something tight. Someone buttering bread, followed by their close-up, then a cut wider to establish and let the audience know where we are. Or maybe a key goes in a lock, a character in close-up checks to see if they're alone, and we cut wide as the door opens. This is a nice little trick; for those few fleeting shots, the audience doesn't quite know where we are in time or space. It keeps them on their toes and therefore involves them a little more in the film. Starting with a wide shot of each scene can be quite boring and pedestrian. Of course the audience will only take so much disorientation, so make sure you cut to the wide or do something to let them in on what's happening (and where) shortly after.

CUTTING DIALOGUE

I start cutting dialogue line for line; when someone speaks, we see them speak. Then we cut to the other person speaking and see them on screen. Then you can go back and trim the gaps and make other adjustments. Some lines may be striking, and I wonder what the other character makes of that delivery. So then I scroll through to their take, and find their reaction. It's exciting to see it come together.

Once you've cut line for line, you can then begin to tweak and finesse. Maybe the scene plays better if we only hear the lines from character B and stick with character A on screen since it's their point of view. This is where reviewing the shots before you start cutting comes in handy. You can overlap the sound and picture, so we might start to hear character B before we cut to them; the video is lagging behind the audio of the scene for a second or two. These are called audio advance or video advance cuts. In the digital world on a keyboard, they're known as "J" and "L" cuts. The letters stem from how the timeline looks having the audio start before the picture, as it kind of looks like a "J," and the opposite with the video starting before the audio kicks in, which looks like an "L." This editing technique is done by unlocking the audio and video sync in your editing timeline. Normally when you trim a clip, the video and the audio will be cut together in sync. To perform these types of cuts, you must unlock the sync. You can then trim the video on its own, backward or forward, independently of the audio.

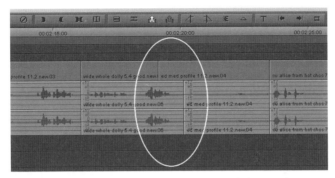

7.1 An edit timeline with the incoming video track starting before its audio

This style of editing is good for a number of reasons. Cutting the video and audio together back and forth on each line can give the scene a pace. This fast cutting works well in scenes involving an argument, for example, as those hard cuts really make those scenes work. By using "J" and "L" cuts, however, the editor is able to slow things down, and this is what the scene might need. The video lagging a second or two behind the audio softens the cut and makes the scene slower. This type of cutting can be used within the same scene, and also as an intro to the following scene; we hear a disembodied voice before cutting to whom is speaking.

SEEING FACES

Seeing the faces of characters as they speak gives them credence. You're telling the audience: "Look here. This character has something important to say." Seeing their face allows for empathy and compassion. Steven Spielberg took advantage of this when he made *E.T.* (1982). None of the adults in the film, apart from the main character's mother, got face time. We saw their bodies from the waist down and heard their voices, but never saw their faces. All of the adults were authority figures, and by not seeing their faces, we didn't identify with them. This film was meant to be from a child's point of view so we, the audience, never saw the adults either.

Consider this example: Maybe we have a character who's rambling and whining. If we decide to focus on the other characters in the scene and only hear the whining off screen, then this helps us to identify with the characters having to listen to the same old ramblings. If what the rambler was saying had any importance, we would see them in shot and therefore be offered an opportunity to relate to them.

WHEN TO CUT

Directors and editors sometimes like to show off their cuts. The best editing occurs when you don't see the "invisible" cuts. Some editors get footage and it's cut cut cut! But what if the scene plays very well for performance and pacing on that nice two shot? You might not need the two singles and extreme close-ups that were also given to you. However, once in the edit suite, you feel that as you kept the cast and crew around past wrap time to get those shots, you have to use them. It's good to realize that sometimes you have to get out of the way of the film. When it takes on a life of its own, recognize it and help it along. If in your gut you feel you don't need those extra shots, then don't use them. Sometimes in the edit, the film "speaks" to you; it becomes a living thing. Recognize these moments. Scriptwriters often tell of the moments when some characters decide what they are going to say for themselves. An editor sometimes has a similar feeling, and instantly knows how material should be cut. Listen to this.

Alfred Hitchcock spoke of the reasoning behind his approach when cutting. If he had two people on a wide or two shot talking casually about something, and they began talking about the plot or some piece of information that took the scene up a notch, that would be the moment to cut to the single shot or a different angle. The cut elevates the dialogue and separates it from the previous lines. So be careful about going into the close-ups too soon during the edit, or you'll have nowhere to go emotionally when the scene does need to go up a gear. If you're already on the close-up when the characters are talking about something benign, then when it really gets heavy, the emotional intensity will be lost.

EDITING –

APPROACH AND THEORY

In the second part of the directing chapter, we talk about juxtaposition. Juxtaposing images side by side is what editing is all about. Each shot has its own meaning, but when the two are cut together, a third meaning is created. Soviet filmmaker Lev Kuleshov demonstrated his theory of montage and juxtaposition in the 1920s by setting up his shots of a man's "neutral" expression intercut with a bowl of soup, the symbol of a cross, and a woman. The audiences read and projected their own thoughts of hunger, sorrow, and love onto the man's face when we cut back to him after seeing the shots of the middle images.

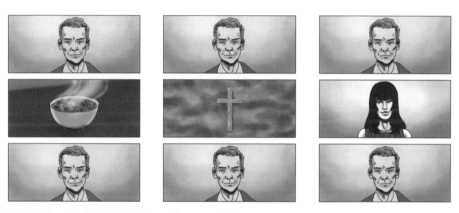

7.2 Soviet filmmaker Lev Kuleshov's theory of montage and juxtaposition in action

I like to call this a "3-shot montage." In the early days audiences had to be taught this technique since the grammar and mechanics of film editing were just in their infancy. Filmmakers and others in media know how to assemble shots so that the audience thinks they are making up their own minds about what is happening. You are creating the third meaning via the juxtaposed images, and are being heavily manipulated into thinking those thoughts.

Here's a nice little trick: When we cut back to the third shot of the actor's reaction, you might decide they need to look horrified, or scared, or joyful. You could merge shots 1 and 3 together and then show the second shot. So the edit is normally "action, then reaction" but instead we now have "reaction, action." Shifting the order like this involves the audience a lot more. For those dangling few seconds they're left thinking, "What is the character looking at? What has caused such a big reaction?" Then the third shot appears, and we are let in on the action.

CUTTING ON ACTION

Back in the early 1900s, directors like D.W. Griffith established the basic grammar of film and knew the psychological power the "cut" held. Griffith made films such as *Birth of a Nation* (1915) and *Orphans of the Storm* (1921), and he fashioned the "invisible cut." By having the invisible cut or cutting on the action of the actor, audiences could be emotionally involved in the story and not be distracted by a choppy cut. Editing became an invisible craft.

Cutting on action means cutting together two shots, perhaps a wide and a medium, or a single close-up and a reverse single close-up, on the moment someone performs an action. This could be when a character takes a drink, opens a door, turns to walk away, or gets up from a chair. This gives the audience the subconscious impression that all events are unfolding in real time. To cut back to a wide shot *before* someone performs an action could suggest that the camera was prepared for the imminent action, therefore breaking the reality of the piece.

When cutting on action, sometimes an exact match can be the wrong point to cut. What? *That doesn't make any sense!* I hear you say. Well, it does. Editing versus what the brain sees and computes is a funny thing. You sometimes need to roll on a frame or two on the incoming second shot. In the split second one shot cuts to the other, the brain allows for the action it's following to have moved on a little. If you cut to the exact match on the incoming shot, it may appear you've rolled back farther than the end position in the first shot! The mind can allow only so much, and you find you can get away with a lot in between the cuts. I've had edits before where someone has their hand up by their face when talking, and in the next shot it's down by their side. I've found a point to cut in on the second shot when arms are shifting or moving somewhat, and this "movement," when cut next to the previous shot, gets merged in the brain to resemble the hand lowering! It shouldn't work, but it does.

The emotion of the scene is the most important part, not the exact position of the actor's hands! When the audience is fully involved in the characters, most of the time they don't even notice mismatched cuts.

You have to be confident you understand the "rules" in order to break the rules. You first have to establish that style, or the standard style, in order for it to work. If you don't, it could come off looking like a bad cut. A good edit is when the emotional and technical aspects coincide.

RULE OF THREE

Most things work better in ones or threes, whether it's story points, shots, or actor's actions. This can be applied to anything. How many establishing shots of the city do you need? Try one, but if the pace is too quick, go for three. Three is a good dramatic number. Two makes the audience feel that both shots are important even if they're not. Four is boring and repetitive. How many times should a character fail at something before succeeding? If they crack the password or open the safe on the first attempt, it was too easy. Two is still easy, and we don't feel much elation when they succeed. Three, however, is enough for us to feel their struggle, and then celebrate their accomplishment. Four gets boring, and we then start to feel that the character is a little useless. Shouldn't they have solved it by now? Whether they will ever crack the problem at hand is uncertain, so our feelings go past the point of empathy and association.

CUT! CUT! CUT!

Most things are better when they're shorter. I had this experience on one of my old films. It involved two strangers, a man and a woman, meeting in the train station. They're chatting about late trains, weather, and they're getting on well. Once on the train, the man asks the woman on a date, and she agrees. Then we cut to the woman getting ready to go out on a date and talking to her best friend about what happened. All this was working well. In the edit suite, my producer said, "How about if we cut the middle scene where he asks her out?" Immediately I knew this was the right thing to do. Now we went from her waiting at the station directly to getting ready. By cutting the middle scene on the train itself, the audience becomes more involved; we have to catch up a little. How did he ask her? How did she react? We're now curious. The missing scene could also make the conversation feel a little more special or private. This worked better on many levels, and the more levels on which an edit or line succeeds, the better. The character is a little mysterious since he did it behind the audience's back. He snuck the question in when we're weren't watching . . . If we later find out that the man was the villain and it was all part of his plan to do her harm, it could make him appear more devious. From a production standpoint, what else have you gained? A day of filming and planning that shoot on a moving train! *If we had thought of this in the script stage, it would have saved us a lot of time . . .*

Sometimes you have to cut your film down for time, maybe to meet a festival or broadcast restriction. However, when doing so, consider this great quote from *Alien* editor Terry Rawlings: "Most of the things to go when they think it's too long are the subtleties." This is important to remember since by cutting shots, you might be trimming time from the length of the film, but you're also trimming what makes the characters tick or what gives the film its magic. Cutting character entrances and exits saves you time, but cutting subtle glances, touches, and character beats could be damaging the piece. Make sure you know the difference.

CHAPTER 8

Three Secrets of Filmmaking

"A lifetime in movies is the same as a lifetime in any profession: you are constantly a student. Every film has different obstacles to overcome."

— CLINT EASTWOOD, ACTOR / DIRECTOR

Here are the three secrets of filmmaking. They could be the three secrets of mastering any discipline. They're called "secrets," but they're not particularly sexy. Over the years and ideally for the continuing future, these three aspects have helped me. I always push them on my students. Those successfully attracting work and jobs, whether paid or not, were already implementing these three secrets. The others made less effort to incorporate them into their work practices.

What are they? Well . . .

One is practical
One is academic
One is personal

THE FIRST SECRET IS
TO FILM AS MUCH AS YOU CAN

Everything and anything. Weddings, short films, music videos, conferences, plays, promos, events . . . When I was younger, I used my family's video camera to film my bedroom. Just pans around the room, close-ups on my books and videos, the cat, etc. No real reason, just practice. But I was learning the equipment inside-out.

I was also practicing craft. How to pan smoothly, what a good frame looks like . . . I've mentioned my early shorts featuring my friends chasing me through the woods that usually ended in a big fight. Well, what we were inadvertently teaching ourselves was orientation, screen direction, shots, feeling, light levels, etc. It's amazing how many of today's filmmakers haven't done some version of this. So get out there this weekend and make a film. A home movie of your town, a music video, or just shots of your bedroom! Anything! Every discipline affects the others. Tattoo that behind your eyelids.

I could be on a job now and something will crop up on set that I know how to solve only because I messed it up 25 years ago on those experimental films.

THE SECOND SECRET IS
TO READ AS MUCH AS YOU CAN

Self-education is critical!

We have the secrets and knowledge of film at our fingertips, yet not everyone reads. Don't come up with any excuses about the cost of books; you afforded this one! Some of my students complain about $40 books then blow that amount on one weekend's alcohol. Used books are also available through eBay, Amazon, and the library! I've read many books on lighting, directing, editing, producing. Make notes, then put them into practice. This is the golden key. I don't know what your chosen speciality is, or even if you have one, but read everything. You want to be a director? Read up on directing . . . and editing. One helps the other . . . gobble up knowledge in all forms. Books, magazines, videos, articles, and blogs are all rife with helpful information.

THE THIRD SECRET IS
TO GET YOUR SHIT TOGETHER

What does this include? Everything that is YOU. When I get emails from students looking for work littered with spelling errors, grammar issues, and font changes, obviously having been cut and pasted from a template, their spelling and letter-writing deficiencies ensure a nonresponse. Or maybe it's your appearance you need to rethink. How presentable are you? Your lack of experience didn't cost you the job; it was your appearance and manners at the interview. Politics is 50% of this business. I and other colleagues know very talented people who haven't been asked back for the next job. Why? Because they were difficult to work with or know-it-alls. You also need to be more self-aware on set. No phones, no loud laughing, no big opinions. People are watching; how do you come across?

You must take care of yourself. How can you survive 16-hour days shooting, driving, and concentrating if you don't eat well, sleep well, and exercise well?

How's your timekeeping? Why are you always late? If you're late to set two days in a row, you won't be invited back for a third. If there are two buses headed to set and one gets you there five minutes before you're due, and the other 30 minutes beforehand, which bus will you take? I had one student do a dry run the day before a shoot so she knew where the location was and how long getting there took. Genius! You don't want to be ringing the producer 15 minutes after call time on the first day of shooting asking for directions. Remember: 95% of the stress we have we brought on ourselves. We haven't prepared; we didn't do the homework; we left too late; we didn't get 'round to making that important call. Small things make big differences.

What areas might you improve upon? Make a list and implement these changes. It will all add up. And it won't just affect your film work, but the other areas of your life, too.

Go to everything; sign up for everything. Courses, seminars, shoots, meetings, networking events, screenings. Everything! Everyone who's succeeded can trace it back to something. "I'm only on this big job because I worked on that other, smaller film with Steve, who recommended me to Claire from the BBC, who knows me 'cause I shot a free video for her sister after meeting her at a film screening . . ." You never know who you will meet and where . . .

Another aspect of this secret is to adopt the "no-excuses philosophy." We all like to make excuses as to why we haven't done something or forgot to do something. I'm as guilty of this as anyone! Identify the excuses you make and work to stop doing so. In most cases the number-one excuse is . . . time.

But time isn't really the reason; it's just that the thing you had to do wasn't a big enough priority for you to go ahead and do it. Everyone in the world, from Richard Branson to Steven Spielberg to Hillary Clinton to the average person on the street, has the same amount of hours in a day. If every day you get up 30 minutes earlier and go to bed 30 minutes later, you have just bought yourself seven hours a week. That's seven hours reading time, essay time, scriptwriting time, editing time, or even time to do housework so it doesn't interfere with your film work.

When students proclaim: "I didn't have time . . ." I respond, "So if a friend's life depended on you completing your assignment, or if that finished essay or script were worth $15,000, *then* you couldn't have done it? You would have lost the money and let your friend die?" If you *had* to make the time, where could you? Could you consider not watching Netflix for the whole of Sunday? Could you not go out partying Friday *and* Saturday? Don't try and find the time; make the time.

I have worked with over 1,000 students, and I can now faithfully spot the signs of those who will go on to work in the industry and those who won't. Some people are very good at being told what to do but lack internal drive or initiative. Some people take notes in class; others don't. Some turn up on time; others don't. Some students hand in their assignments on time; others offer excuses about printers running out of ink. Years later, students who applied themselves are now working on the new TV show; the ones that didn't still work part-time supermarket jobs. Which one will you be?

CHAPTER 9

Common Traits of Student Films

"Each time I view my work after a film is finished, I only see the mistakes."
— JEAN-PIERRE JEUNET, DIRECTOR

Most (if not all) filmmakers have produced films that they are not proud of. Our first efforts are where we try new things, learn the craft, and copy what we have seen in our favorite films.

Here is a list of common traits some student films share that might be worth avoiding or at least knowing why you're using them. Students often believe their film is the first to contain a brave, new style, but these sins have been committed by most filmmakers, who ideally clear their system of them by the time they're professionals. I'm no exception. I was guilty of most of these, so hopefully this list will help you avoid the same pitfalls.

2.35 ASPECT RATIO

We've all seen epic, large-scale sci-fi or action films using this widescreen aspect ratio. It was chosen to benefit and enhance the storytelling and not used arbitrarily. What makes a film look expensive is the action on screen, not the screen itself. Consider this aspect ratio carefully before committing to it. If you do decide to use this frame, make sure it is planned and shot accordingly, rather than cropping the image in post and losing half your frame.

BLACK AND WHITE

Black and white has always had the connotation of meaningful arthouse films or film noir. Shooting in black and white can be a powerful tool, but again ask what

157

your reason is for choosing it. From a cinematography perspective, it might be wise to decide beforehand that you will be converting to black and white so that the lighting choices can help separate people and locations when shooting. You'll no longer have the use of color to help determine separation or depth.

LENS FLARE
Yes, lens flare can look good, but it's not the be-all and end-all of cinematography. Use it sparingly.

GETTING HUNG UP ON GEAR, RESOLUTION, OR TECHNOLOGY
If you have the option, the established workflow, and the hard-drive space, shoot with the best resolution you can. If that happens to be 4K, go for it. Be aware of the means, workflow, and other significant implications of shooting 4K; don't just do it because you think it will somehow make your film better. Don't let the tail wag the dog here. If it will cost you more to shoot 4K, consider diverting that money to better production design, visual effects, or whatever else might need attention. Shooting with a popular camera doesn't mean the film will be any better. It might be what the last James Bond film used, but if you don't know where to put the camera or how to shoot good images, that's all moot. Focus on the story and characters, not the hardware and software. Pixels don't matter; good stories do.

DIRECTORS TRYING TO BE NEW AND DIFFERENT WITH STRANGE AND OBSCURE CAMERA ANGLES
In my student days, we were guilty of this one. I think the strangest place we put the camera was the inside of a baked-bean can! As to why the camera was in there, we couldn't tell you. It was a time of trial and exploration, though, and some directors just want to show off. Don't think you have to draw attention to yourself or the camera. A camera is sometimes best placed at eye level, in front of the action, not spinning around from the ceiling.

PROJECTS THAT ARE TOO AMBITIOUS
Sometimes a film works best in our heads, where we can see all the great set design, wonderful costumes, and fancy props. However, you simply don't have the means to

pull it off. I've read scripts set in the dystopian near future or in alternate worlds, and the necessary resources just aren't there. I am not encroaching on anyone's creativity, but understand what can be achieved successfully with your budget. Is it better to write a contemporary film where audiences can get immersed in the drama, or try for futuristic high spectacle that forces them to immediately make concessions?

THE GUN-BARREL-DOWN-THE-LENS SHOT
Don't. It was a cliché 25 years ago and is even more so now.

NO DEPTH TO SHOTS OR FILMING AGAINST PLAIN WALLS
Depth is something we discussed in the directing chapter. Stage and block your scenes so you have a foreground, midground, and background to your shots. It helps orientation, shows off your lovely location, and looks more pleasing to the eye. If you're forced into a plain corner of a set, can the background be broken up with a picture frame or plant? Could the action shift a little to the left or right so the window is in the frame?

OVEREXPOSED SHOTS
On low-budget projects, you may not have the lighting equipment required to control and manage your exposure. If there are elements of your frame that are blowing out or overexposing in an environment you can't control, restage the shot accordingly. This could be as simple as your actor taking a step back, or panning the camera a little to the left.

TOO MANY EDITS OR INSERT SHOTS
Just because you shot four angles of the action doesn't mean you have to use them all in the edit. Let the pace of the action on screen tell you when to cut. I've see many student films with cuts every two seconds covering a simple action. It's a chance for people to show off their camera skills and editing skills, but the real talent lies in knowing what to use and when. The camera operator may have supplied you with a nice pull focus from the plant to the actor's face, but cut it if it disrupts the pace or takes the audience out of the film. Having inserts or cutaways of benign actions or objects are also a staple of the student

film, like hands picking up a teacup in close-up only for the audience to see that the character has done that in the following shot. Unless it is an important piece of business that we need to see in close-up, don't force it in the edit just because it was shot.

SWEARING FOR THE SAKE OF IT

Another one that my filmmaking colleagues and I were guilty of. Yes, Tarantino has swearing in his films, so does Scorsese; but, like they used to tell you at school about smoking, it's not cool, kids. Use it when appropriate rather than thinking it makes your film more adult.

YOUNG ACTORS PLAYING OLDER

Having your 16-year-old friend play a 35-year-old police detective is cute, but doesn't work on film. That character needs some weight. If you need older actors, use them. This is where your resourcefulness comes in. Who do you know? Who do they know who can help you?

POOR AUDIO

A classic. We've all seen films with wind rustling on the soundtrack or low, inaudible mumbling from actors who have their back to the camera or are off-mic. Hire a good sound recordist or restage the action so your microphone picks up the sound. Monitor the audio with headphones so you know when you've got it and when you need another take.

DREAM SEQUENCES OR FLASHBACKS

Dream sequences and flashbacks can work if done and timed well. But they are seldom warranted and are used to conceal script weaknesses. A character jolting upright after a nightmare is also a tired cliché.

HAVING LONG, MEANDERING EDITING TO SUGGEST MEANING

Audiences have short attention spans. Longer-than-necessary shots don't add weight, just bore the pants off us. Stanley Kubrick might have gotten away with it, but still, don't. Meaning comes from story and theme, not shot length.

CHAPTER 10

Final Thoughts

"Film directing is synthesis: the product of countless choices. Filmmaking is will plus technique plus vision. But your vision is the most important."

— Paul Greengrass, director

Whenever I finish a teaching session, I normally end on something very similar to the following, so I might as well finish this book the same way.

I've tried to cover everything I can within these pages: every personal experience, every tip, every mistake, and every success. We've looked at the technical aspects, the approaches, and the styles. We've turned inward to recommend personal considerations that will benefit those entering the industry. Take all this information and run with it on your own filmmaking endeavors.

We've talked about passion, drive, keeping high standards, and taking action, but also about learning and absorbing as much as you can. Learn the basics, the structures, the technical processes, and other people's approaches. Develop your own technique by reading, watching, listening, and *doing*, whatever field you're in. This way you build up an immense vocabulary, which is so important. What you have read, watched, and listened to augments your own tastes, producing a unique voice and set of influences. Your writing, lighting, or directorial style will be a combination of the technical knowledge you've learned, the blogs or magazine articles you've read, the films you've watched, the YouTube tutorial videos you've viewed, and your own life experiences and ideas. They all add up to produce work that holds itself to a high standard and is inherently you.

In his book *Outliers*, author Malcolm Gladwell writes about success and people who have achieved it. Gladwell says it takes 10,000 hours to become really good at something, whether it's music, dancing, writing, football, or filmmaking. The 10,000 hours entail not only practice, but time spent reading, watching, and gathering the life experiences that will define your work and make it special. In the Secrets of Filmmaking chapter, secret number one is to shoot as much as you can and this would build up your 10,000 hours. See what you like, copy that style or approach, move past it, tweak it to be more you, and get all the clichés, rip-offs, trials, and experiments out of the way. The remains distilled from getting everything out of your system is then your work. On set I can access that personal approach immediately, not questioning why something doesn't work or if I like it. I know instantly. There's a confidence to be had in this new mindset, but to reach this stage quickly and transcend the experimental phase, *shoot*.

Years in the industry prove that knowing and strengthening your own mind is key. Dealing with criticisms, lack of response, rejection, attack from outside, or your own self-doubt and negative talk is all par for the course. So absorb all the information you can. Those feelings of doubt, rejection, and attack aren't reserved for people who haven't "figured it out" yet; they're commonplace. Even those at the top of the film business are subject to criticisms and assaults. It's not about eliminating those aspects, the self-doubt, or being so technically proficient as to avoid them; it's about strengthening your mind to live side-by-side with them every day. Uncontrolled, your emotions can cripple you, stop you from daydreaming new ideas, or prevent you from finishing your film. Countless producers, directors, and filmmakers, even on big Hollywood productions, experience these same feelings. It's okay to make mistakes!

There really is no one right way to enter the film industry; each person has their own path, and no one way is the same as the next. Some go to film school, others don't; some work for production companies full-time, others freelance. But thinking ahead, both in private and on set, is the skill most widely shared and sought after by film professionals.

When I'm speaking with students they often inadvertently reveal that their biggest obstacle to getting something made is not gear, the idea, or money, but them. They need to get out of their own way. Whenever an idea or suggestion is made to go make or write something, prohibitive obstacles always seem to present themselves. The old excuses and insecurities come up. Most of the time I discover, as they do, that they know more than they realize and it's just fear that's stopping them. *What if I mess it up? What if people don't like it? What if . . . ?* You could ask: *What if people do like it? What if it comes together really well? Where could that lead to?*

So go make films. Go write. Go shoot. When is the best time to start that process? I'll let you answer that one.

Sources

CHAPTER 1

Quentin Tarantino quote from *Cutting Edge: The Magic of Movie Editing* documentary

CHAPTER 2

Dawn Steel quote from her *They Can Kill You . . . But They Can't Eat You: Lessons from the Front*

CHAPTER 3

Peter Suschitzky quote from *FilmCraft: Cinematography* by Mike Goodridge & Tim Grierson

CHAPTER 4

Sidney Lumet quote from his *Making Movies*

CHAPTER 5

Guillermo del Toro quote from *FilmCraft: Directing* by Mike Goodridge
Steven Spielberg quote from *The Making of Raiders of the Lost Ark* 1981 documentary
Joe Wright quote from *Atonement* DVD director's commentary

CHAPTER 6

Ted Tally quote from *Screenwriters' Masterclass*, edited by Kevin Conroy Scott
Paul Newman quote from *Paul Newman: The Craft of Acting* featurette on *The Verdict* DVD

Anthony Hopkins "Honking and hooting" quote from Scott Hicks interview on *Hearts in Atlantis* DVD

Anthony Hopkins "Stillness" quote from "Inside the Labyrinth" interview on *The Silence of the Lambs* DVD

Anthony Hopkins quote on Ridley Scott from *Breaking the Silence: The Making of Hannibal* DVD

CHAPTER 7

Terry Rawlings quote from *Dangerous Days* documentary

Pietro Scalia quote from *Rise and Rise Again: Making Ridley Scott's Robin Hood* documentary

CHAPTER 8

Clint Eastwood quote from *FilmCraft: Directing*

CHAPTER 9

Jean-Pierre Jeunet quote from *Moviemakers' Master Class* by Laurent Tirard

CHAPTER 10

Paul Greengrass quote from *FilmCraft: Directing*

SCREEN GRABS TAKEN FROM THE FOLLOWING FILMS:

Watch Over Me — CBA Productions DVD
Jurassic Park — Universal DVD
Dances With Wolves — TIG Productions DVD
The Judge — Warner Bros. DVD
Die Hard With a Vengeance — Cinergi Blu-ray
Robin Hood: Prince of Thieves — Warner Bros. Blu-ray
The Pledge — Morgan Creek Productions DVD
Atonement — Universal DVD
It's a Wonderful Life — Universal DVD

About the Author

Paul Dudbridge is a British director, producer, cinematographer, and educator, making feature films, television, commercials, and music videos.

Paul started producing at the age of 11 when he convinced his father to shoot his first short film. When the resulting footage didn't match what he had seen in his head, Paul went behind the camera. Making films — directing, scripts, shots, and angles — has been in his blood ever since.

With over 20 years' experience in the business, Paul has numerous film and television credits to his name. His first broadcast credits include producing and directing ITV's *The Christmas Storybook*, featuring legendary actor Joss Ackland, as well as directing music videos for MTV. His work as a cinematographer includes the action thriller *By Any Name*, based on the bestselling book by Katherine John. As a producer and director, he helmed the science-fiction series *Horizon*, which won awards at several international film festivals and earned Paul a Best Drama Director nomination at the Royal Television Society (West of England) awards in 2016.

When not filming, Paul guest lectures at various universities and colleges around the UK. Most recently, he ran the Writing and Directing module for the master's course at the University of Bristol; taught Cinematography at Falmouth Film School; and gave Lighting for Drama workshops for BECTU, the UK's media and entertainment trade union.

When he's not making or watching films, Paul enjoys reading, chess, fitness, Eastern philosophy, and has just taken up surfing.

He lives in Bristol, UK.

Contact Paul via email at paul@hanoverpictures.co.uk.

{ THE MYTH OF MWP }

In a dark time, a light bringer came along, leading the curious and the frustrated to clarity and empowerment. It took the well-guarded secrets out of the hands of the few and made them available to all. It spread a spirit of openness and creative freedom, and built a storehouse of knowledge dedicated to the betterment of the arts.

The essence of the Michael Wiese Productions (MWP) is empowering people who have the burning desire to express themselves creatively. We help them realize their dreams by putting the tools in their hands. We demystify the sometimes secretive worlds of screenwriting, directing, acting, producing, film financing, and other media crafts.

By doing so, we hope to bring forth a realization of 'conscious media' which we define as being positively charged, emphasizing hope and affirming positive values like trust, cooperation, self-empowerment, freedom, and love. Grounded in the deep roots of myth, it aims to be healing both for those who make the art and those who encounter it. It hopes to be transformative for people, opening doors to new possibilities and pulling back veils to reveal hidden worlds.

MWP has built a storehouse of knowledge unequaled in the world, for no other publisher has so many titles on the media arts. Please visit www.mwp.com where you will find many free resources and a 25% discount on our books. Sign up and become part of the wider creative community!

Onward and upward,

Michael Wiese
Publisher/Filmmaker